Studies in Sociology

Edited by

PROFESSOR W. M. WILLIAMS
University College, Swansea

6

SOCIAL STRATIFICATION

STUDIES IN SOCIOLOGY
Edited by Professor W. M. Williams

published

in preparation

SOCIAL STRATIFICATION

James Littlejohn
University of Edinburgh

LONDON . GEORGE ALLEN & UNWIN LTD
RUSKIN HOUSE MUSEUM STREET

First published 1972

ISBN 0 04 301051 2 Hardback
     0 04 301052 0 Paperback

Printed in Great Britain
in 10 on 11 point Plantin type
by Unwin Brothers Limited
Woking and London

CONTENTS

p. 85 line 22 from the top:
Not "*un*usually" but "usually"

p. 110 line 9
Not "schools" but "suburbs"

p. 110 line 15
"nation" not "notion"

p. 112 line 14
Not "previous" but "this"

p. 61 line 7 from the bottom
"planes" not "places"

p. 117 2nd line from the bottom
"supply of power" not "supply or power"

p. 120 2nd line from the bottom
"employments" not "employment"
and "characteristic" not "characteristics"

p. 126 line 2
"realms" not "healms"

p. 127 line 19
"on" not "of"
and "child's" not "child"

p. 128
There is a line missing after line 26
The sentence should read:
"The two are of course ideal types of mobility, but there is
no doubt that the English system resembles the former and
that of the U.S.A., though only for its white population,
the latter."

p. 131
Footnote No. 5
The name is "Worsley" not "Warsley"

I

Theory

SOCIAL stratification is the name under which sociologists study inequality in society, i.e. the unequal distribution of goods and services, rights and obligations, power and prestige. These are all attributes of positions in society, not attributes of individuals. Individuals are unequally endowed as regards, for instance, health, strength and I.Q., but such differences do not provide the data from which studies in stratification start, although as we shall see later sociologists are interested in knowing to what extent and in what way individual differences in health and I.Q. are associated with the social inequalities which are our object of study. No sociological training is required to observe many of these latter differences—everyone knows that wages in some occupations are low and salaries in others high, that Cabinet Ministers have more power than ordinary citizens, that doctors enjoy higher prestige than dustmen and so on. Most of us are indeed naturally curious about these differences and adopt some attitude towards them. In this respect sociologists are distinguished from fellow citizens only in wanting more, and more exact, information.

However, sociologists also want to know how these differences arise, what differences in behaviour are associated with them and what consequences for society follow from them. Simply collecting information on distributions of socially valued rewards or on deprivations is not what most sociologists mean by the study of stratification. When they say of a society that it is stratified they are referring to a feature of the structure of that society, and they mean that the society exhibits significant breaks or discontinuities in the distribution of one or several of the attributes mentioned above, as a result of which are formed collectivities or groups which we call strata. For example, of our own society we sometimes say that it has an upper class, a middle class and a working class. It is the relations between or among such strata, and the relation of the system of relations formed by the strata to institutional complexes, such as politics or education, in which the sociologist is primarily interested.

Sociologists have distinguished several general types of stratification. A major distinction has been formulated by T. H. Marshall as follows. On the one hand are systems in which the difference between one stratum and another is 'expressed in terms of legal rights or of established customs which have the essential binding character of law. In its extreme form such a system divides a society into a number of distinct, hereditary human species—patricians, plebians, serfs, slaves and so forth. Stratification is, as it were, an institution in its own right, and the whole structure has the quality of a plan, in the sense that it is endowed with meaning and purpose . . .'.[1]

On the other hand is the kind of system which is not so much an institution in its own right as a by-product of other institutions; strata

'emerge from the interplay of a variety of factors related to the institutions of property and education and the structure of the national economy.'[2]

Within the first of these general types sociologists have distinguished a few subtypes, particularly systems of estates and of castes, and some sociologists include as a distinct type those in which the most important discontinuity in the distribution of rights is that between slaves and freemen.[3] Estates are strata distinguished from each other through differential immunities defined in law, e.g. immunities regarding taxation, or the kind of court in which the individual can be tried. A stratum of slaves is from some points of view an estate, since the important distinction between a slave and a freeman is that the former does not, or only to a limited extent, enjoy the protection of civil courts. However, as a particularly dramatic example of stratification we may consider slavery separately from estate systems. Caste denotes a kind of stratification most conspicuously, and according to some authorities exclusively, associated with Hindu society, in which the differences between strata are defined in the first instance in religious terms by degrees of purity and impurity.

Under the second heading come those systems of stratification characteristically found in industrial democracies such as our own. Societies exhibiting the previously described types of stratification are characterized by their acceptance of a general norm of inequality. People do not subscribe to the proposition that all men are equal, or at least not to the extent of ensuring that all are equally placed with regard to the law, or of allowing that all have equal access to grace or purity. Societies exhibiting the types under the second heading accept a general norm of equality and some, such as America, write it into their constitution. The norm is a major element in the modern conception of natural law, or natural right, which Weber defined as the sum total of all those norms valid independently of, and superior to,

[1] T. H. Marshall, *Citizenship and Social Class*. Cambridge (1950), p. 30.
[2] Ibid., p. 31.
[3] See, for example, T. Bottomore, *Sociology*. Allen and Unwin (1964), p. 179.

any positive law, and which provide the very legitimation for the binding force of positive law, for example, those laws which confer on all citizens the right to dispose of their private property or their labour without interference,[1] or the right to vote.

Marshall's distinction in effect distinguishes stratification in industrial democracies as a separate type from all others, and there are good reasons for doing so. First because there stratification is a result of the interplay of a variety of institutions in a social milieu where it is asserted that all men are equal; not a goal, a plan or a blueprint to which social relations are made to conform by legal sanctions. Second because industrial democracies are more complex in structure than estate or caste societies; in the former the division of labour has proceeded further, there are many more roles making up the social structure, institutions to co-ordinate roles and groups proliferate, and there are extensive population movements. Hence stratification in industrial democracies is a more complex field of study; strata are less easily identified, or rather they cannot be identified independently of the methods sociologists use for the purpose. I shall outline these methods below, and the theories associated with them.

When a society exhibits stratification it means that there are significant discontinuities in the distribution of goods and services, or of property, rights and obligations. Analogously, different types of stratification mean that there are significant discontinuities between the systems of stratification exhibited by various societies. Any general theory of social stratification must deal in some way with the second sort of discontinuity. There are, broadly speaking, two main directions in which explanation may proceed. In one the various types are shown to be stages in a process of development; in the other the types are treated as only variations of the same thing, i.e. of the same elements and processes present to a varying degree in all cases, or modified by factors extrinsic to stratification itself. Of the two general theories of stratification, the Marxist and the functionalist, the former proffers a solution of the first sort, the latter of the second. The two are not absolutely different in the respect indicated, but differ markedly in emphasis. In addition to these two theories we shall consider notable contributions to our understanding of the subject from Max Weber, and some ideas of Thorstein Veblen.

As indicated, Marx's theory of stratification is not something distinct from his theory of society and its development, and his leading hypothesis, his 'guiding thread' as he called it, he formulated in an oft-quoted statement:

---

[1] Subject to non-violation of basic freedoms. One cannot for example enter into a contract of slavery. Weber's view of natural law and its modifications in modern, twentieth-century society is expounded in *Law in Economy and Society*, Cambridge (1954).

'In the social production which men carry on they enter into definite relations that are indispensable and independent of their will; these relations of production correspond to a definite stage of development of their material powers of production. The totality of these relations of production constitutes the economic structure of society—the real foundation, on which legal and political superstructure arise and to which definite forms of social consciousness correspond. The mode of production of material life determines the general character of the social, political, and spiritual processes of life. It is not the consciousness of men that determines their being, but, on the contrary, their social being determines their consciousness. At a certain stage of their development, the material forces of production in society come in conflict with the existing relations of production or, what is but a legal expression for the same thing, with the property relations within which they had been at work before. From forms of development of the forces of production these relations turn into their fetters. Then occurs a period of social revolution. With the change of the economic foundation the entire immense superstructure is more or less rapidly transformed. In considering such transformations, the distinction should always be made between the material transformation of the economic conditions of production which can be determined with the precision of natural science, and the legal, political, religious, aesthetic or philosophical (in short, ideological) forms in which men become conscious of this conflict and fight it out.'[1]

By forces or powers of production Marx means knowledge about the natural world, technology, energy (including human labour power), and the effective deployment of these in specific organizations such as plantations or factories. By relations of production he does not mean the day to day relations between persons at work as studied at present by industrial sociologists, nor does he mean the division of labour in society. He means the relation between classes of persons marked off from each other by differential rights and obligations with regard to productive property, in the simplest case between owners and non-owners of productive property. In bourgeois (industrial democratic) society the relation, between capitalists and labourers, includes, for instance, the right of property owners to exclude non-owners from use of their property, and their obligation to pay wages to those they employ; the numbers of individuals in each class; and their conflicting interests, the owner's in keeping wages as low as possible, the non-owner's in raising the level of wages.

Forces and relations of production have altered in the course of social development through, Marx thought, more or less clearly defined

---

[1] K. Marx, preface to *A Critique of Political Economy*.

stages. The stages he proposed are the primitive, the ancient, the Asiatic, the feudal and the bourgeois.[1] These stages accord to some extent with the classification offered above of types of systems of stratification, ancient society being characterized by the division between masters and slaves, feudal by the division between landlords and serfs, and bourgeois by the division between capitalists and labourers. The primitive stage is characterized by the absence of classes. These four stages comprise the history of the West to date. The next stage will be the socialist one which, like the primitive but on a higher level of complexity, will be marked by the absence of 'the antagonistic mode of production'. Here the state will wither away to be replaced by the 'abstract administration of things'.

The Asiatic stage is peculiar to the Orient and has two main features:

(a) an organization of production in the village by castes, each specializing in an hereditary occupation;
(b) domination of large territories by a state consisting of a despot and a bureaucracy, often controlling large-scale irrigation projects.

The relation between the two is one of simple extortion of tribute or taxes from villagers by the state bureaucrats. Because the village is a self contained unit of production and exchange it can survive through the endless wars of rival despots and the fall of dynasties; because it is self contained, yet loses its surplus production to the bureaucracy, further development of society is blocked, hence the stagnation of oriental society as compared with the West. The hypothesis of a social system in which bureaucrats commanded by a despot exploit a working population has proved irresistible to some anti-Marxist or anti-Soviet scholars, with the result that the literature on the subject of oriental despotism is largely polemical.[2] In Chapter 4 on the caste system I shall ignore this aspect of the matter and concentrate on modern studies of local caste systems.

Marx did not write a history of development in the West, although he sketched out his ideas on the subject. There are two main strands of thought in these ideas. According to one:

'The history of all hitherto existing society is the history of class struggles. Freeman and slave, patrician and plebian, lord and serf, guildmaster and journeyman, in a word, oppressor and oppressed, stood in constant opposition to one another, carried on an uninterrupted, now hidden, now open fight, a fight that each time ended,

[1] K. Marx, *Precapitalist Economic Formations*, tr. J. Cohen, ed. E. J. Hobsbawm. Lawrence and Wishart, London (1964).
[2] See K. Wittfogel, *Oriental Despotism*, New Haven (1959). Also R. Aron, *Main Currents in Sociological Thought*. Pelican, London (1968).

either in a revolutionary reconstitution of society at large, or in the common ruin of the contending classes.'[1]

Linked with this are ideas about the nature of development as a process such as those quoted above: development requires that there be a contradiction between forces and relations of production, bringing a class conflict to the point of revolution. The sort of situation Marx had in mind was the French Revolution, or the nineteenth-century phenomenon of massive unemployment,[2] strikes, and violent suppression of workers' attempts to organize. Proper utilization of this vast productive force of workers and equipment required that the means of production be socialized, put into operation for the benefit of all and not the enrichment of a few.

These ideas constitute the last satisfactory strand in Marx's expositions, as many Marxist scholars admit.[3] It is clearly a gross simplification to say that all previous history is the history of class struggles. Moreover, Marx never demonstrated what exactly had been the contradiction in ancient society or in feudal society, while the development from primitive to ancient he thought had been accomplished simply through enslavement and conquest[4]—surely no contradiction there.

The other strand is an outline of history as a gradual clarification of the human condition. According to this view social development has consisted since antiquity in a gradual polarization of unequal positions, so that in nineteenth-century bourgeois society all the issues connected with inequality in society become concentrated into a clear cut opposition between capitalists and proletariat. Society had to develop to precisely this point before the possibility of socialism offered itself and before the concepts requisite for the clarification of the human condition and for directing society's transformation to the next stage should become available.

These concepts were first formulated, Marx thought, in bourgeois political economy, which he regarded as the anthropology of capitalist society, the bourgeoisie's account of man, his nature and place in the world. Thus it starts from a conception of man as a producer (not, for example, as a child of God) exploiting natural resources, and of men as exchanging products, i.e. of society as a system of exchange. It

[1] K. Marx and F. Engels, *Communist Manifesto*. Penguin, Harmondsworth (1967), p. 1.
[2] See E. P. Thompson, *The Making of the English Working Class*, Gollancz, London (1963).
[3] See Hobsbawm's Introduction to Marx's *Pre-Capitalist Economic Formation*, op. cit.
[4] Also according to Engels, through dramatic changes from matriarchal to patriarchal organization as a consequence of changes in the dominant forms of property. See his *Origin of the Family, Private Property and the State*. London (1942).

assumes as a natural state of affairs the institution of private property and an equally natural desire in men to acquire it, and it takes for granted that in acquisition and exchange each individual competes with the others to maximize his gains. Through the division of labour, itself stemming in part from the institution of private property, different individuals perform different functions in the process of production, distribution and exchange. For analytical purposes these functions can be classed as contributions of land, labour and capital; the product of this collaboration, the commodity, is sold in the market at a value determined by the forces of supply and demand, and from which the three functions receive proportionately their respective rewards of rents, wages, and profits.

The system so operating expressed a kind of necessity, it corresponded to human nature, the bourgeois thinkers held. This first formulation, however, Marx maintained was inaccurate, because the bourgeois thinkers mistook a particular culture (their own society) for a natural state of affairs. They had not learned the lesson of history, study of which informs us that past societies have committed themselves to some very different institutions from those we consider proper, right or even tolerable. Men have lived and died believing in the justice of, for example, slavery or in the truth of astrology. Faced with the diversity of norms in the graveyard of history we might conclude that justice and truth are illusions, necessary perhaps for the continuance of society but not anything for a wise man to trouble himself about. This conclusion is uncomfortable to live with, and for the most part men adopt the same attitude as the bourgeois thinkers that one's own society is the necessary state of affairs because it is in conformity with human nature.

We can, however, also conclude as Marx did (and many other nineteenth-century thinkers) that while previous epochs or stages were mistaken about themselves, and the present not wholly clear about itself, nevertheless history is essentially a development towards some absolute norms and that there is a true human condition and a possible state of social affairs corresponding to our nature as humans. The true human condition must of course be hidden from men in the stages anterior to its realization, hence their accounts of themselves have always been wrong. Their accounts have been partly a product of ignorance and partly an expression of, and justification for, relations of production in their respective societies. We can chart their errors by comparing what they had to say about themselves with the true human condition, which can be summed up in the formula 'labour is the source of all value'. This only becomes clear when society attains the stage of development in which labour and capital stand opposed to each other as the two dominant categories in terms of which the productive process can be analysed. In the following paragraphs I shall outline Marx's methods and the main results of his analysis of bourgeois society, interpolating an account of this second conception of development.

His main aim was to disclose the 'law of motion'[1] of capitalist society. He meant by this phrase that one and the same process explains the emergence of capitalist society from feudal society and accounts for the main features of the former, particularly class conflict. In accordance with his leading hypothesis he looks for this process in the relations of production in capitalist society, the relation between capital and labour. In borrowing these categories from economics Marx is not embarking on an economic analysis of society. He is constructing a model of society by abstracting from empirical detail the key social relations, which, once understood in conceptual purity can be used to explain the empirical facts. The model is applied to particular social situations, for instance nineteenth-century England, and progressively modified as more and more empirical data are brought within the scope of analysis. Capital and labour are represented empirically by capitalists and workers. Capitalists are those who own, i.e. have sole rights to access to and disposal over, the means of production. Workers are those without these rights; they are dependent on the former for access to the means of production and must enter into an exchange with them. The exchange takes the form of the capitalists buying the workers' labour for money. The analysis of exchange as a social relationship is the core not only of Marx's analysis of capitalist society but of social development, and goes under the name of the labour theory of value. To understand this theory we need to understand his analysis of 'the commodity'.

A commodity is something produced by work or labour which is subsequently exchanged for something else, in capitalist society for money. Marx's analysis of the commodity starts from the observation that the outstanding feature of capitalist production is that all production is of commodities, i.e. production is with a view to selling (exchanging) the product in a free market. In previous epochs most production had been either for direct use (the producer himself consuming or using his own product), or else had been production within a context of relations in which persons could exchange directly. By this Marx means that most of a wide range of transactions were effected without the use of money and normally the persons were involved in continuous relations of a sort including more than merely exchange of goods. For example, peasants on a feudal manor gave so many days' labour to the lord of the manor in return for rights to cultivate land and to protection in his court. The emergence of capitalist production is coextensive with the full emergence of the commodity as the sole object of production. How did this situation arise?

[1] K. Marx, *Capital*, vol. I. Foreign Language Publishing House (1956).

Marx analyses the history of the commodity as logical steps and not in terms of men's motives for exchanging. He wants to show what is logically entailed in exchanging, that is to exhibit the necessary conditions of the possibility of exchange and of the existence of commodity production. For the first step we assume the simplest possible exchange of objects, A for B. Logically this means that:

(a) each object considered separately has a use value, which is the physical form of the object. For instance, a stone axe head is useful because it is sharp bladed and compactly heavy, a spear because it is sharp pointed and its weight dispersed in extension.

(b) Considered together each has an exchange value, i.e. the other object. The exchange value is what the use value is not. This contradiction has to be resolved for exchange to be effected; or rather, men act before they think and exchanging resolves the contradiction. Implicit in the act is a reduction of the two disparate utilities to a common factor by reference to which they can be equated. This factor can only be the human labour congealed in the objects.

> 'It is the expression of equivalence between different sorts of commodities that alone brings into relief the specific character of value-creating labour, and this it does by actually reducing the different varieties of labour embodied in the different kinds of commodities to this common quality of human labour in the abstract.'[1]

The next step is simply the extension of the initial conditions to include most produced objects. These are equated in various proportions, $1A = 2B = \frac{1}{2}C$, etc. Entailed here are the following:

(a) most labour must be considered the same;

(b) since labour is undifferentiated, the magnitude of the value embodied in a product must be the amount of labour required to produce it.

The situation represented by the second step is for various reasons unstable. The final step requires that the value of all commodities be expressed in terms of one single commodity, i.e. money. With this, produced objects become commodities in the full sense of the term. Again Marx stresses that he is not analysing motives; he is not saying that men invent money in order to make all commodities commensurable. On the contrary it is because exchange discloses all commodities to be of varying magnitudes of value, i.e. realized human labour, that they become commensurable. Hence their values can be

---

[1] K. Marx, *Capital*, vol. I. Foreign Language Publishing House (1956), p. 50.

B

measured by reference to one special commodity set apart for the purpose of measuring. The entailments relevant to social relations here are:

(a) that all the products of labour take the form of commodities, i.e. are produced for the purpose of exchange;

(b) that labour power itself becomes a commodity, is sold in a free market, and hence that relations among men become relations among commodity owners;

(c) that exchangers must see each other as free and independent owners, i.e. as each having the right to dispose of his product.

(d) that the idea of human equality acquires 'the fixity of a popular prejudice'.[1] This is required as conceptual support for the acceptance of human labour power as undifferentiated.

An implication of this which Marx often stressed is that the modern conception of natural law, according to which all men are equal, is the intellectual formulation of, or disclosure of meaning in, the most general relationship among men which has come into being with the widening scope of commodity production, the extension of the market, and the freeing of labour from particularistic ties to manor and guild, since late feudal times. Commodity production, universal use of money, belief in human equality, and conscious apprehension of labour as the source of value all entail each other. Consider now the history of the commodity in relation to the stages of development.

In the primitive era there is no private property. The environment is seen as a sort of divine gift and thought moves only in mystical images and religious symbols. Kin groups each produce what is necessary to satisfy their own wants. There is sharing but no production for exchange within the tribe. Accordingly, Marx thought, the commodity must first appear where community life ends in intertribal or inter-community exchange.[2] This first flickering of the message of human equality is however extinguished by the second stage. One group enslaves another, a transition prepared for by a kind of slavery latent in the family which is seen in the rule of a patriarch over wives and children. What happens in slavery is that one group appropriates not the labour of others but their complete persons, thus turning them into natural conditions of their own existence. Private property appears

---

[1] K. Marx, *Capital*, vol. I. Foreign Language Publishing House (1956), p. 60.

[2] Some studies of primitive economic systems lend support to Marx's hypothesis. See R. Salisbury, *From Stone to Steel*. Cambridge (1962). Some other studies, however, would seem not to support the hypothesis. See L. Pospisil, *Kapauku Papuan Economy*. New Haven (1963). For discussion of various issues involved see essays in ed. R. Firth, *Themes in Economic Anthropology*. Tavistock, London (1967).

among the dominant group as each individual's share of the communal property, land, slaves and animals; the state as a specific type of organization now emerges partly out of the needs of war or slave raids and partly out of the solidarity of freemen against slaves, as institutions to control them and administer conveyance, inheritance and protection of property. The aim of production here is man in the form of master or aristocrat, not commodities to be sold for money. Precisely because the aim of production is the (best) citizen, and labour power remains hidden in the person of the slave, the thinkers of the ancient world, despite their brilliance, never arrive at a theory of value, at political economy. The actions of the slave and of free citizens are incommensurable. Perception of the true human condition that labour is the source of value, which is only apparent where genuine free exchange occurs, escapes them. Despite a fairly advanced division of labour and a certain amount of trade, production and commerce are despised, conducted largely by foreigners, slaves and freemen. Thought still moves to a great extent in religious terms, only now the gods are at war with each other, reflecting political strife among rival lineages attempting to dominate the state. Inequalities are distributed in disparate dimensions which cannot be brought together in sharp focus: slaves and freemen, debtors and creditors, patricians and plebians, engage in conflicts that come to no resolution.

Note the course of the analysis here. Marx is not saying that Roman masters first thought of turning other men into natural conditions of their own existence and subsequently to achieve that end proceeded to enslave them. Men act before they think, they enslave others because they see that so doing furthers their material interests. But having done so, their ideas about the relationship between themselves and their slaves are thereafter generated by the core meaning that slaves are mere natural conditions of their masters' existence, like draught animals, whether or not the masters apprehend the core meaning. In fact in Roman law slaves were treated in the first instance under the rubric of the law of things, not of persons, and the slave was defined as 'the speaking instrument'.

A major difference between this and the feudal stage is that whereas in the former the city is the centre of social, political and economic life, in the latter social organization largely reverts to unities tied to rural localities such as fiefs, manors and village communities. Most production is by serfs tied to particular units whose seigneurs extract as much as they can from peasant production, using it to maintain petty courts and retinues of armed men who can be used to keep serfs in their place. The serfs' situation is not quite that of slaves, but the forced direct exchange of labour, services and produce in the feudal domain continue to prevent men from arriving at a true understanding of labour, value, sources of inequality and so on. The current level of men's incomprehension of themselves and society is as always reflected in the dominant ideology, the hierarchical orders of the angels under God mirroring and justifying the social hierarchy. A new conflict, between secular and sacred orders, church and state, distracts society. Production in such towns as there are is organized in much the same relationships as in the countryside and each guild is a closed group in which masters more or less have possession of the persons of apprentices and journeymen.

The dissolution of this system of production throws up the elements of the next. Kings in their struggle against feudal landowners ally themselves with, or make use of, the merchants and in any case further the interests of the latter. They also manage to have the private armies of the former disbanded. Further, as a result of enclosures many peasants are forced off the land. Towns receive those peasants expelled from feudal organization and in towns they become free, in the sense of not being tied to particular masters or social units. There they are employed as wage labourers, that is merchants and master craftsmen buy their labour, not them as persons. It is cheaper simply to buy labour when required. So begins the dissolution of the relation of production under which labourers are a mere element in the objective conditions of production.[1]

'For capital the worker does not constitute a condition of production but only labour. If this can be performed by machinery, or even by water or air, so much the better. And what capital appropriates is not the labourer, but his labour, and not directly, but by means of exchange.'[2]

Trade revives; the Reformation, by bringing to the forefront of consciousness the problem of free will prepares men for the free market, and the bourgeoisie grow in wealth by the process of capital accumulation.

This is 'the law of motion' of capitalist society, a process unleashed within the relationship of exchange between one who owns the means of production and one who owns only his own labour power which he is free to sell wherever he feels he will derive the most advantage from the transaction. Recall here that the value of a commodity is the amount of labour embodied in it, the socially necessary labour time required for its production. Now labour at a certain level of technological sophistication, certainly in nineteenth-century Europe, quickly produces enough to maintain itself. That is, it soon in the course of a day's work

---

[1] These remarks are merely illustrative. There are numerous detailed studies of the process. Some useful references are: E. A. Kosminsky, *Studies in the Agrarian History of England*. Oxford (1956). Barrington Moore, *Social Origins of Dictatorship and Democracy*. A Lane, London (1967).

[2] K. Marx, *Pre-Industrial Economic Formations*, op. cit., p. 99.

produces a value equivalent to what the worker needs to purchase food, shelter and to remain alive in good or at least adequate health until the next day. An hour or two's work is sufficient. This, the value of labour, is the workman's wage. However in order to earn it the worker has to go on producing for as many hours as the capitalist directs. By the end of the day the capitalist has appropriated from the worker a value in excess of the latter's wage, a surplus value. This he converts into money by sale of the worker's production, which adds to his stock of capital for reinvestment. Note that this is a theory about social structure, not a moral condemnation of the bourgeoisie. Each of them has to obey the law of motion of capitalist society or be driven out of business by competition from the others. Each has to keep wages at the level of the value of labour otherwise his costs of production will be higher than that of his rivals, and his commodities will be priced out of the market. The private interest of each is the interest of his class. Similarly with labourers. Suffering from the effects of exploitation they associate in unions to engage in conflict with their employers, demanding higher wages, or shorter working hours, and so on.

History for Marx is the history of the gradual extrication of the commodity and of exchange from involvement in coercive relationships, as in slave and feudal societies, and of the extrication of production from relations of personal domination and subjection, with the consequences mentioned above for freedom and equality in society. Marx praised the bourgeoisie for their accomplishments yet condemned as merely formal and as a mockery for the labourers the freedom and equality they claimed to have won for them. Labourers were merely wage slaves in actuality, exploited and alienated both from the products of their labour and from society itself. However, the bourgeoisie had now brought into focus and polarized all the facets of inequality and had made it plain that inequalities all flowed from the opposition between property owners and labourers. Marx considered that the polarization would continue, that capitalists would become richer and labourers poorer by contrast, until revolution and reconstruction opened the next era.

For Marx political organization was not something distinct from social structure. In bourgeois society the state is as always merely the institutional form of the existing distribution of power, the de facto power of the capitalist over the worker. The state as an apparatus of control and enforcement is in the hands of representatives of the capitalist class, who see to it that the interests of their class are promoted and protected. Government is a committee for managing the affairs of the bourgeoisie.

Although in his model Marx has only two classes, when he came to apply it to the contemporary situation he added others as the facts required. He distinguished various kinds of capitalists, i.e. the petit bourgeoisie (e.g. shopkeeper) from the bourgeoisie proper, craftsmen owning their own tools from labourers, and the lumpen proletariat from the proletariat. The lumpen proletariat are those members of the proletariat who become mercenaries of the bourgeoisie, the police and soldiers who use strong-arm methods to keep the proletariat under control. Marx also recognized that in many parts of Europe the peasantry was or could become a class of some political importance.

Marx was fully aware that his model was a model, an abstraction he himself had conceived for the purpose of gaining understanding of social processes. He was also fully aware that few workers saw society in the terms that he did. They suffered but did not conceptualize; they engaged in sporadic local rebellion against particular conditions, but did not organize, to any great extent, a revolution to destroy the whole system. Many were unaware of the true source of their misery and did not recognize that their true interest lay in uniting with other members of their class to resist and overthrow the bourgeoisie. Marx distinguished here between class-in-itself and class-for-itself by reference to the absence or presence respectively of a consciousness of common interests among those composing a class. Later Marxists spoke of false consciousness to account for the often observed fact that many individuals in a class-in-itself, so far from comprehending their common true interests, i.e. their material interests as Marxists conceive them, act in a way contrary to their interests. For example, labourers often vote for a political party committed to the protection of private property in the means of production. One of the main tasks of the communist party that Marx founded was to bring the proletariat to a true consciousness of its position. It is in these terms that the author of a recent study of the making of the working class in nineteenth-century England speaks of class as 'an event',[1] meaning the arrival on the part of those n a common position at a true consciousness of it.

Weber

There is some controversy among sociologists as to Weber's relation to Marx, whether he completed the Marxist analysis or whether he offered a different one. Certainly like Marx he treated stratification as a phenomenon closely linked to the distribution of, and struggles for, power. In this regard Marx and Weber differ from modern functionalists. However, Weber also differed considerably from Marx in several respects; in his conception of power, in his assessment of the course of European history, and in his conception of what constitutes a satisfactory explanation in sociology. First let me outline Weber's ideas on the subject of stratification.

Weber distinguished three types of social formation relevant to the

[1] Thompson, op. cit.

study of stratification: class, status groups and parties.[1] Classes appear in the context of market situations and the basic categories, he agreed with Marx, are property holders and non-property holders. Within these two categories classes may also be distinguished by source or amount of income, such as rentiers and industrialists, or skilled and unskilled workers. Weber's main point in that classes, as distinct from status groups, are collectivities distinguished from each other by a differential position with regard to a market wherein they compete to maximize material gain. In this situation thought pre-eminently takes the form of rational calculation.

Status groups, in a variety of senses which Weber devoted some effort to exploring, stand opposed to class. This is basically because they arise out of a situation which hinders the strict carrying through of the market principle, i.e. the principle that a man, or what he offers, is valued in terms of the laws of supply and demand in an open market. Status groups belong to the sphere of social honour and are distinguished in the first place by varying degrees of prestige. In this sphere thought on a mundane level is concerned with standards of propriety, consumption and taste and on a deeper level with judgement as to the ultimate values by which one should regulate one's behaviour. For example, preferences for asceticism or sensual luxury, care for other-worldly interests or mundane material interests, or concern with the formulation of ideals and sometimes with quite new life goals. At particular times and places the two spheres, the market and social honour, may conflict, as when priests forbid usury between coreligionists. In such a situation a pariah group, such as the Jews in medieval Europe, may become notorious for moneylending at rates of interest. Compared to classes, status groups are more conscious of themselves as an entity, and the members of a status group participate in a common style of life, subscribe to common ethical standards and at times strive to realize exalted ideals. In the most clear cut cases a status group distinguishes itself by restricting or prohibiting social intercourse and marriage between its member and other groups,[2] for example the whites of the USA in relation to negroes.

Relations between status groups and classes are intricate and various. A status group may include persons of differing class membership, as with both whites and negroes of the USA, while a class may contain several status groups.[3] An occupation by its nature may promote the elaboration of particular values, standards and pursuits into a distinct life style, as with the knights of the Middle Ages. A status group may use its prestige to shore up a weakening economic position, as the Junkers of Germany managed to do for some generations.[4] Generally

[1] M. Weber, *Essays in Sociology*, trs. Gerth and Mills. Routledge, London (1948), pp. 180–95.
[2] Ibid., p. 300.   [3] See Chap. 5, p. 109.   [4] Weber, op. cit., p. 300.

speaking, wealth confers prestige, and high status requires wealth to support it, but there are many exceptions. Poverty accepted as an ethical or religious task may confer high prestige.[1] As a general rule, Weber held, stratification by status is the normal situation in periods of economic and technological stability.

'Every technological repercussion and economic transformation threatens stratification by status and pushes the class situation into the foreground. Epochs and countries in which the naked class situation is of predominant significance are regularly the periods of technical and economic transformations. And every slowing down of the shifting of economic stratification leads, in due course, to the growth of status structures and makes for the resuscitation of the important role of status honour.'[2]

The distinction between classes and status groups is in principle easy to comprehend, but it is important to understand the scope of its significance in Weber's sociology. He was not in any sense absolutely opposed to Marx as he agreed for example that

'present day society is predominantly stratified in classes',

although adding

'and to an especially high degree in income classes',[3]

and that the issue in the present-day class struggle is the price of labour. The scope of his disagreement with Marx as regards interpretation of history is indicated by his remark that

'In the past the significance of stratification by status was far more decisive (than classes) . . . above all, for the economic structure of the societies.'[4]

Marx himself was aware, as the outline of his account of slavery shows, that classes in nineteenth-century industrial Europe comprised a very different social structure from those of previous epochs. However, as Ossowski has recently pointed out, he altered from time to time the terms by which he characterized modern classes, speaking of, for example (in addition to capitalists and proletariat), those who work and those who do not, of those who employ hired labour and those who do not.[5]

Examples of these can be found in many non-modern societies.

---

[1] See Chap. 4 on the caste system.
[2] M. Weber, *The Theory of Social and Economic Organization*. Collier-Macmillan, London (1947), p. 193.
[3] Weber, op. cit. (1948), p. 301.   [4] Ibid., p. 301.
[5] S. Ossowski, *Class Structure in the Social consciousness*. Routledge, London (1963), chap. 5.

Moreover, simplifying drastically in the *Communist Manifesto*, he implied that classes throughout history could be conceived of as oppressor and oppressed. As a result, less in the major writings of Marx than in those of his epigoni,[1] the distinctiveness of previous epochs was effaced and the whole course of history assumed to be governed by a struggle between classes. It was to this levelling of the uniqueness of previous epochs and of other existent civilizations that Weber objected, and to the view that the past could be interpreted in the terms most relevant to the interpretation of the present. The open market as the matrix regulating allocation of resources and value, determining which occupations will flourish and which die, is a creation of capitalism. In non-capitalist societies status groups compete to establish the superiority of particular world views, and to monopolize economic advantages, for example the right to taxes or levies.

Consider now the difference between Weber and Marx in relation to problem setting and method. Marx held that: (*a*) men until his day, and most even then, were unaware of the true human condition; (*b*) that history had as goal the realization of a society adequate to it, the classless society; (*c*) that European society had developed to the point that the goal was almost attained. It follows that men, in extending their command over nature and in their political struggles of the past and present, have been unaware of the true meaning of their own actions. Marx conferred meaning upon, and explained social action by, reference to these premises and to his notion of material interest as developed in his theory. By the time Weber was writing, economists had discarded the labour theory of value central to Marx's analysis,[2] and he felt there was no call to think that there is *a* human condition, but to the contrary there are only innumerable human situations. Nor could Weber believe that history had any particular goal, certainly not a goal in the form of a particular form of society. Some implications of this for the kind of problem Weber set himself are as follows. Clearly he could not treat non-capitalist societies as merely exemplifying incomplete development, to the contrary they realized other possibilities as regards values, life goals and organization. The question then arose why capitalism emerged precisely in Europe and nowhere else. Weber used other civilizations, particularly India and China, as contrasts by which to ascertain what was distinctive about the history of Europe. This involved study of the dominant status groups of these civilizations, Brahman priests and Confucian scholar-administrators, and of the consequences of the values and ideas promoted by their

---

[1] S. Ossowski, *Class Structure in the Social consciousness*. Routledge, London (1963), chap. 5, p. 127. Ossowski remarks that in a letter to a periodical, towards the end of his life, Marx warned of the danger of applying generalizations applicable to capitalist society to other periods of history.

[2] See J. Schumpeter, *Capitalism, Socialism and Democracy*. N.Y. (1950).

respective religions for everyday and for specifically economic behaviour. That of the Brahman, for example, stressed the importance
of other-worldly concerns, thus devaluing activity in this world except in
so far as it contributed to other-wordly ends.[1]

The implications for his methods of Weber's general approach are
various, particularly in relation to his definitions of social formations
and the kind of explanations he held to be valid in sociological studies.
Clearly he could not disclose meaning in social actions and institutions
(which were the deposit of past social actions), or explain their
appearance in such and such a society by reference to a supposed
goal of history or to the supposed process by which it is gradually
achieved, a goal and process not apprehended by men. Weber was well
aware that social action often brings about results unintended by the
actors, but in his view one cannot explain the action by unintended
results. On the contrary, one must show why the action did have the
results that it had. In his view men act to achieve goals and the first
task of sociology is to arrive at an understanding of why they choose
one set of goals rather than another. Understanding proceeds by
relating goals to the dominant values in society, or the values stressed
in the styles of life of competing status groups. These styles of life may
conflict as much as the interests of class, or forces and relations of
production, in Marx's analysis: for example, a religion which enjoins
humility is hardly likely to be acceptable to a warrier aristocracy.
However, struggle among status groups to enhance and preserve styles
of life and associated prestige is not endemic in society, though a major
task of sociology is to show how in a particular society one comes to
dominate the others.

Weber brought party into juxtaposition with class and status mainly
to bring into relief, by contrast, some general characteristics of the
latter two. A party has an explicit program and a staff of officials to
ensure continuous implementation of it. Classes and status groups have
neither. There are bases from which communal actions may arise, but
not necessarily, or if they do, with any necessary regularity of incidence
and aim. Consistent with these views, Weber refused to treat society
as a process in the third person, or to treat social formations as if they
were substances with fixed and permanent properties. His definitions
of social formations are designed to delineate the situation of individuals
rather than to construct elements of a model of a total society. He speaks
of class and status situations thus:

'We may speak of class when (i) a number of people have in common
a specific causal component of their life chances, in so far as (ii) the
component is represented exclusively by economic interests in the
possession of goods and opportunities for income, and (iii) it is

---

[1] See Chap. 4.

represented under the conditions of the commodity or labour markets.'[1]

Similarly, a status group is a number of people for whom some life chances are determined by the social honour accorded them. The concept of life chances has proved fruitful for study of various aspects of stratification in modern society (see pages 118–36 below).

These various strands in Weber's approach are all illustrated in his famous study of the connection between the spirit of capitalism and the protestant ethic.[2] What was distinctive in European history, he thought, was a process of rationalization apparent in all or most spheres of culture and society, a discarding of mythic thought and of reliance on magical techniques combined with a sober attention to mundane tasks at the expense of other-worldly interests so prominent in some religions. The discarding of myth and magic applied not only with respect to attitudes to and treatment of nature, but with respect to social relations and conduct. Examples are the abandonment of divination or of trial by ordeal in law cases, or the rejection of techniques for inducing trance or dissociation as a means of attaining a state of grace. A more modern example would be the change in the last two generations in our attitude to gypsies, the change from regarding them as untouchables with mysterious powers to regarding them, as do Manchester University students, as unfortunates in need of elementary education.

Calvinism, a decisive moment in rationalization in religion, was particularly important for the emergence of capitalism. One of the main features of the latter was steady application to the job on the part of all involved in production, labourers and artisans as well as capitalists. This contrasted with attitudes to work in other societies, where the custom was to work only sufficiently to be able to satisfy unvarying traditional needs, or to devote to work only such time as could be spared from festivals and feasts. In the Middle Ages, for example, it has been calculated some hundred and fifty-six days in the year were holy, non-working days. Calvinism promoted both steady application to work and also to capital accumulation in the following way. Calvinists were concerned about the question of grace or salvation, whether God had chosen one for eternal bliss in heaven or otherwise, yet communication with God they held to be impossible. They rejected the idea that mediation between God and man was possible through priests. In this situation Calvinist divines recommended that as God had given us the world to use we should accept the tasks of ordinary life in the spirit of thankful performace of divinely ordained duty.

---

[1] Weber, op. cit. (1948), p. 181.

[2] M. Weber, The Protestant Ethic and The Spirit of Capitalism, tr T. Parsons. London and N.Y. (1930).

Work should be a calling, as the Catholic priest's duties were, though one's performance would not influence God's choices. But success in worldly tasks might be interpreted as a sign of God's favour. Life should be devoted to the calling, and frivolous use of time, as in entertainment, avoided. Money should not be spent on ostentatious living as that too was a distraction from the main issue. Those who were successful in accumulating money accordingly simply reinvested it in productive enterprise. The Protestant ethic appealed particularly to the status group of burghers or town citizens and its various successes were bound up with their subsequent fortunes in different parts of Europe.

Weber's thesis on the connection between the protestant ethic and the spirit of capitalism initiated one of the major intellectual controversies of the century.[1] This does not concern us here; what does is that by this and many other studies Weber showed that status constitutes a dimension of stratification distinct from, though involved with, that of class, not only in the past but also in modern society.

A simplified statement of Weber's contribution to the study of stratification is that he showed that it manifests itself in three main dimensions, class, status and power, and that the strata in these dimensions in a given society need not necessarily coincide. His analyses of power, domination and the process of legitimization by which a dominant status group becomes accepted as dominant, are too extended and complex to summarize here. However, one conclusion he arrived at is very relevant to any consideration of the development of stratification in modern society and it is a view which has since come to be widely appreciated. It is that whether a modern society socialized its means of production or not relations of domination within it would remain largely unaffected. The modern industrial enterprise and the modern state, he pointed out, secure continuous production and administration by means of bureaucratic organization. In this the dominated accept the dominators on the basis of legality, of concensus on the rules and procedures concerning the selection and limits of the powers of the latter. This is opposed to the kind of acceptance found in pre-industrial society, based (apart from times when naked coercion is employed) on traditional respect or allegiance to charismatic leaders. Weber held that modern bureaucratic organizations, whether in capitalist or socialist societies, are sufficiently similar as to entail common problems for the two types, for example the problem of maintaining morale among the dominated. Alienation would not cease when the state withered away to be replaced by the abstract administration of things. The point has been incorporated in what is sometimes now called the theory of convergence. Briefly, it is that socialism and capitalism are two routes to the same end, the modern industrial

[1] R. W. Green, *Protestantism and Capitalism*. Boston (1959).

society, and however much two societies differ at the beginning of their journey in the respects indicated by the two terms, they will be much the same by the end of it.

Veblen's contribution[1] to the study of stratification is slighter than those of Marx or Weber, but he dealt with topics which in modified form, and under the name of the theory of embourgeoisement, have recently been the subject of examination by some European sociologists. His thesis is that in a wide range of societies, including modern, the relations between upper and lower classes is not one of class struggle; to the contrary it is one of imitation or emulation of the upper by the lower. Marx and Engels had noted that the British working class seemed more concerned with acquiring the standards of living and life style of higher classes than with revolutionary activity and even when enfranchised large numbers of them voted for the Tory party. They thought this was due to Britain's success as an imperial power, for exploitation of colonial populations not only provided the British working class with a higher standard of living than they would otherwise have enjoyed, but also prompted them to ally themselves with their own ruling class against the former.[2]

Veblen's theory is this. The struggle to accumulate wealth has long since passed the point where it is a struggle for sheer subsistence or even for a minimum of comfort. The motive at the root of accumulation of wealth and property is now emulation. Possession of wealth confers honour and even the poor now vie with each other for social status through small increments in wealth. The rich of course set the pace and their rivalry is conducted in terms of a norm of conspicuous consumption, by which they must demonstrate their position by abstention from productive work, lavish expenditure and in general by non-productive consumption of time, as for example by their learning of dead languages, by the niceties of interior decoration, by elaborating a ceremonious and time wasting code of manners, by indulging in useless sports like hunting, and in opulent hospitality. Their standards set the standards of excellence for society as a whole, and the lower classes, far from attempting to destroy their masters are, in comparing themselves with them, overawed by them. They conceive themselves to be inferior to them and accept their lower position or attempt to achieve a vicarious satisfaction in imitating them, aping their manners, buying inferior products of a general type of which the rich have the best, or participating, in a less expensive way, in their pursuits. The public enclosure at Ascot is not the royal box, but one can still watch the sport of kings from it. On the theme of embourgeoisement see pages 140-3.

[1] T. Veblen, *The Theory of the Leisure Class*, N.Y., Viking Press (1931).
[2] See J. H. Goldthorpe *et al.*, 'The Affluent Worker and the Thesis of Embourgeoisment,' Vol. 1, no. 1, 1967. Cambridge.

Conspicuous consumption has become part of the general vocabulary of sociology, though few sociologists would apply the concept so liberally to the culture of the upper classes as Veblen did. However, he brought to our notice the importance of status symbols in the process of legitimization (in Weber's terms), and called attention to the corruption of culture involved in the process in his lifetime. Then, industrialists, financiers, and the rich and powerful in general vied with each other in having mansions built in styles borrowed from the past, set their wives and daughters to 'artistic' pursuits while hordes of servants prepared and served ceremonious meals, and generally demonstrated their inability to create new status symbols appropriate to the new style of domination they exercised.[1]

The functionalist theory

Functionalists are very much concerned with the problem of integration and equilibrium in society, and in that respect their theory derives from Durkheim.[2] Their theory of stratification reflects that interest, although they also owe much to Weber. The modern statement of the functionalist view of stratification is most prominently associated with Talcott Parsons, though many others such as K. Davis, and W. E. Moore have contributed to it.[3] It is above all a product of modern American sociology. Society is regarded as a system of action, and stratification as a generalized aspect of the structure of all social systems. As action is oriented to goals it involves selective processes regarding them, towards attaining them, and finally towards actors in roles. Hence roles[4] are subject to evaluation. A condition of the stability of a social system is that there be integration of its value standards to constitute a common value system.

> 'Stratification in its valuational aspect, then, is the ranking of units in a social system in accordance with the standards of the common value system.'[5]

The judgements by which a rank order is established may be applied to the qualities, performances or possessions of actors in roles. By

[1] T. W. Adorno, *Prisms*. Garden City Press (1967), pp. 73–95.

[2] A. R. Radcliffe-Brown, *Structure and Function in Primitive Society*. Routledge, London (1952). T. Parsons, *The Social System*. Free Press (1951). R. K. Merton, *Social Theory and Social Structure*. Free Press (1949).

[3] T. Parsons, 'A Revised Analytical Approach to the Theory of Social Stratification', *Class Status and Power*, eds R. Bendix and S. M. Lipset. Free Press, pp. 92–108. K. Davis and W. E. Moore, 'Some Principles of Stratification', *American Sociological Review*, vol. 10, Apr. 1945, pp. 242–9.

[4] Other system units are also subject to evaluation, collectivities of various sorts. For the sake of brevity in exposition, I shall speak only of roles, as indeed do most functionalists.

[5] Parsons, op. cit. p. 93.

qualities is meant position or positions in a social system, or what is more usually called status.[1] Judgements are made in terms of four main types of value standards: (i) technical norms, or efficiency; (ii) achievement norms; (iii) norms assessing contribution to integration, and (iv) norms relevant to socialization. The four types are found in all social systems, but each social system has a distinctive value pattern stressing one or two of the above four types. For example, Soviet society stresses standards (iii) and (i), while American society stresses standards (ii) and (i). We may take as given that different systems exhibit different levels of role differentiation; granted that there is role differentiation in each system, a particular order of roles or a subsystem of roles will be stressed in each in accordance with its value pattern and the rank order of roles here will be particularly important for stratification. Thus in America, where efficiency and achievement are the dominant norms, the strategic subsystem for stratification is the system of occupational roles. A simplified summary of the theory so far is that stratification is the result of two social processes, role differentiation and ranking in terms of dominant values.[2]

How do functionalists conceive the place of power and control of resources in systems of stratification? Parsons sees power as an intrusion into stratification, causing discrepancies to arise between the ideal rank order of roles in terms of values and the actual rank order of roles in a given society. Its intrusion is also responsible for imperfections in integration in systems of stratification. This view is linked with his treatment of possessions (control of resources, property, offices, etc.). Power he defines as realistic capacity to actualize interests, resulting from three sets of factors: (i) evaluation by the common values standards; power conferred in this way has the character of authority; (ii) the degree to which deviance is permitted; (iii) control of possessions. This last he admits

'is inevitably correlated with high status, hence there is a source of power independent of the direct evaluative legitimation of the status.'[3]

What is central in Marx's theory is in the functionalist theory extraneous to stratification, and only relevant to it as disturbing perfect integration.

Yet there is a certain ambiguity in the functionalist conception of possessions for they also link possessions with the notion of reward. Possessions in general are facilities and reward objects, and the functionalist's point is that allocation of facilities and rewards must

[1] On the term 'status' see pp. 47–8 below.
[2] B. Barber, *Social Stratification*. N.Y. (1957), p. 2.
[3] Parsons, op. cit. p. 109.

correspond in some orderly way with the allocation and ranking of roles. The basic principle of optimum allocation would be of facilities to those who can use them most effectively. In other words possessions are both a source of disturbance in systems of stratification, and at the same time are a type of reward essential to integration of these systems. The ambiguity no doubt reflects social reality, but the point in the study of many systems is to ascertain the extent to which possessions, as currently distributed, function in either of these ways.

For functionalists the ultimate reward, and perhaps the essence of all rewards in society, is prestige, or being highly regarded by others. Strata emerge from the process of differentiation and evaluation in the form of social classes, each composed of actors in roles enjoying roughly the same prestige. However, for many functionalists strata as defined above by discontinuity need not emerge from the processes that they consider result in stratification. Stratification may take the form of a continuum of social status, i.e. prestige without any significant discontinuities. At the extreme this view regards stratification, at least in modern society, as a mere distribution of prestige, and strata as simply a classification of the population by levels of social status, the levels being determined by the sociologist for the purposes of each particular research. There are no natural breaks, no clear boundaries, between one stratum and another.

A social class is a number of actors in roles enjoying roughly the same prestige, and a system of classes is a number of these units ranked by differential prestige. The system is multidimensional in the sense that prestige may be awarded on the different grounds of possession, qualities and performances, but unidimensional in the sense that the strata which emerge from the process are differentiated only by greater or lesser amounts of prestige. Each class represents a grade in the application of a common value system to the diverse roles in society. A system of stratification is a series of grades united through consensus on values. If in a particular system there is dissatisfaction with it and alienation from it among members of the lower strata, this is simply because of frustration, because they have been imbued with the desire to attain the most highly rewarded positions, but have been unable to do so.[1]

As an illustration of the type of system of stratification which results when functionalist conceptions are translated into research procedures, we may take the work of W. L. Warner and his associates. They take the local community or small town as the milieu within which to study stratification in America. Their basic procedure is to find out, both by explicitly asking informants and by noting them in conversations devoted to other topics, the judgements which individuals make con-

---

[1] Merton, op. cit.

cerning the relative rank of members of their community.[1] In the same way, categories used in ranking are elicited; the names given to the categories by informants may be formal in character, such as 'middle class', or symbolic, such as 'local aristocracy', or descriptive, such as 'people you look up to'. Informants are also asked to name some families and individuals within the categories they identify. Their replies are matched, and members of the various categories are then examined to ascertain what attributes members of a category have in common, and what different, from members of other categories, and what discontinuities in relationships can be observed between one category and another. From these procedures the researcher constructs a picture of social classes in the community, arranged in a hierarchy and marked off from each other by:

(i) different prestige, upper and lower etc.;
(ii) differential association outside of work relationships, e.g. friendship or marriages are for the most part between persons in the same class; or members of the topmost class meet each other in the Rotary club, those of the lower classes in bowling clubs etc;
(iii) typical differences in style of life, e.g. typical spending habits, reading matter, etc., and in the kinds of occupation pursued, e.g. labouring as against the professions or commerce;
(iv) typical differences in life chances, e.g. in the probability of an individual's attaining a position of local power.

Warner found that:

'Although the voters among the three lower classes far outnumbered those in the three higher, they had a disproportionately small percentage of officers in the political hierarchy. In other words, the upper classes held a greater proportion of the higher offices than their numbers in the voting and general population would by a mere chance allow them.'[2]

Individuals or families may move from one stratum to another as they acquire the characteristic attributes of an adjacent stratum and are accepted as equals by the members of it, although Warner never attempted to measure the extent of this kind of social mobility. The number of classes so located varies from one community to another, but whatever the number such a system of stratification is never simply a reflection in social relations of differences in wealth among families.

[1] W. Lloyd Warner, M. Meeker and K. Eells, *Social Class in America.* Chicago (1949). A concise statement of Lloyd Warner's methods is given in W. Lloyd Warner, 'A Methodology for the Study of Social Class', *Social Structure*, ed. M. Fortes, N.Y. (1949), pp. 1–17. An example of his research results is Lloyd Warner *et al.*, *Democracy in Jonesville*. N.Y. (1949).

[2] W. Lloyd Warner and P. S. Lunt, *The Social Life of a Modern Community.* New Haven (1941), p. 366.

C

In his first study, of a small New England town (population 30,000) with six social classes, Warner found that many members of the topmost class were less rich than many members of the next lower class, but enjoyed greater prestige because their forefathers had belonged to the class for several generations, while those of the latter had not. After considering the results of studies of this sort Warner redefined the phenomenon of class in the following way:

'By class is meant two or more orders of people who are believed to be, and are accordingly ranked by the members of the community, in socially superior and inferior positions'.[1]

The general picture is of a massive concensus concerning social superiority and inferiority, and in contrast to conflict between strata, merely competition among individuals to achieve a higher position.

Warner confirmed that, as is generally agreed among sociologists, the unit of stratification in modern society is the nuclear family, i.e. members of the family share the same status and are evaluated as a unit. He also found that the social attributes of the family which provide the more reliable indices of a family's social status are the type of house it inhabits, the area of town in which it is located, the source of income of the head, his education and his occupation.

We shall consider in a later Chapter the limitations of this approach. Warner did not himself offer any explanation for the kind of stratification he described, but his descriptions provided a starting point for functionalist theorists who are more concerned with explaining the existence of social stratification than with the empirical description of specific class structures.

The aim of functionalist analysis is in general to show the functional necessity for those institutions it examines, i.e. to show how an institution is necessary for the continuance of a social system as an ongoing entity. For Parsons the necessity for stratification arises from any society's having to allocate its members to different positions in its structure, and to motivate them to perform their duties adequately. The clearest formulation of the functionalist explanation has been given by Davis and Moore,[2] and following them, by B. Barber.[3] Stratification fulfils two functions, one expressive and one instrumental, as follows. Positions in any social structure differ in functional importance for society in, for instance, those requiring specialist skills and those not. In the accordance of greater prestige and higher rewards to the more important, society's values are expressed, publicly affirmed, broadcast, and confirmed. Stratification thus contributes to the maintenance of concensus regarding values and hence to social integration since,

---

[1] W. Lloyd Warner and P. S. Lunt, *The Social Life of a Modern Community*. New Haven (1941), p. 82.

[2] Davis and Moore, op. cit.   [3] Barber, op. cit.

functionalists assert, the former is a necessary condition of the latter. The instrumental function is this: individuals differ in ability and capacity, and it is essential that society endeavours to ensure that those more qualified occupy the more important positions, a condition achieved by differential distribution of rewards.

'If the rights and perquisites of different positions must be unequal, then society must be stratified, for this is precisely what stratification means. Social inequality is thus an unconsciously devolved device by which societies ensure that the more important positions are conscientiously filled by the more qualified persons.'[1]

This thesis has been extensively criticized on the grounds that it is untestable and that it is a wholly unrealistic appraisal both of the process of allocation of persons to roles and of rewards to roles, in most and perhaps all societies.[2] In many societies the most valued roles are inherited, as also are possessions, and even where the former process is discouraged, as in our own society, advantages in the process of open competition for valued roles may yet be distributed by a process resembling inheritance (see pages 118–31). Functionalists treat these sources of *de facto* inequalities as another instance of values. They set up a dichotomy between closed and open recruitment into positions and groups, which is also referred to as a dichotomy between ascription and achievement in the allocation of roles. Different societies are known to exhibit one rather than the other course. Now this makes value a most ambiguous concept. For whereas value with respect to ranking is expressed in the judgments of the actors in a social system, value in this latter context is merely a feature of a social system as revealed to the enquiring gaze of the comparative sociologist. An Australian aborigine cannot say whether his society exhibits closed or open recruitment, having no experience of any society but his own. Whether it exhibits one or other, we cannot attribute the characteristic to a consensus on values on the part of aborigines.

The two main or holistic theories, the Marxist and the functionalist, are often contrasted in a variety of terms. Dahrendorf points out that they can be seen as exemplifying two mutually exclusive answers to the question 'how is it that human societies cohere?'. Functionalists stress integration through concensus on values, Marxists stress the coercion and conflict of interests. The former conceive

'of social structure in terms of a functionally integrated system held in equilibrium by certain patterned and recurrent processes',

the latter

'view social structure as a form of organization held together by force and constraint and reaching continuously beyond itself in the

[1] Davis and Moore, op. cit., p. 243.
[2] See eds. Bendix and Lipset, op. cit., 2nd edn (1967), pp. 47–86.

sense of producing within itself the forces that maintain it in an unending process of change.'[1]

For Ossowski they exemplify two contrasting general conceptions of class structure, of each of which several subvarieties are to be found in the literature on the subject, both past and present. The point of contrast is the nature of the relations held to obtain between social classes, 'ordering relations' or 'relations of dependency'.[2] In the first case

'class division is conceived as a division according to the degree of a quality treated as a criterion of class participation'.[3]

That is, any one class in the system (except the lowest) has more of the critical quality than the class immediately below it, and this is the essential feature of relations between or among them. He further distinguishes schemes of simple gradation from those of synthetic gradation, according as to whether ranking of classes is by reference to one objectively measurable characteristic or to several which have no common gauge. An example of the former would be the Roman division of citizens according to the value of the property they owned (see page 53); as an example of the latter Ossowski gives the class divisions of American society as conceived by Warner.

Contrasted to schemes of gradation are those in which classes are held to have different attributes as a result of which they stand in relations of dependence. These can be of two main types: mutual dependence as in the medieval idea of society as an organic whole composed of those who fight, those who pray, and those who work; or dichotomic one sided dependence, in which society is held to be divided into two classes characterized by opposed attributes, such as the propertied and non-propertied in Marx's analysis. Usually one such class is held to be subject to the power of the other.[4]

Lenski sees the two theories as representative of reflections in sociological theory of contrasting political and moral philosophies, the conservative and the radical.[5] Many authors find a conservative bias both in general functionalist theory and particularly in the functionalist

---

[1] R. Dahrendorf, *Class and Class Conflict in an Industrial Society*. Routledge, London (1959), p. 159.   [2] Ossowski, op. cit.

[3] S. Ossowski, 'Old Notions and New Problems,' *Transactions of the Third World Congress of Sociology*. Amsterdam (1956), p. 19.

[4] Ossowski's distinctions seem to me valid and useful, but his discussion of them is in places confusing, partly because some of his examples are ill-chosen, partly because he does not carry his analysis far enough, for example, he admits that from 'another point of view' one sided dependence as in Marxism can also be seen as mutual dependence. He fails to distinguish kinds of dependence, for example (*a*) ontological; X cannot exist without Y, as with capital and labour in Marx's analysis; (*b*) functional; as in the medieval idea; (*c*) logical; statement X implies statement Y, existence not being in question.

[5] G. Lenski, *Power and Privilege*. McGraw-Hill (1966).

theory of stratification.[1] A related, though not identical view, links the two theories to the social milieu in which each has been propounded, a Europe rent by political-social conflict and a USA

'where neither a working class political movement nor a working class ideology has ever become established'.[2]

Another pair of contrasting terms applied in comparing the two are synchronic and diachronic, the former usually with the implication of a deficiency. For example, R. Meyer reviewing Warner's work remarks that the latter's ahistorical approach results in an 'entirely spurious impression of timelessness', for we know that modern societies change continuously, and consequently

'it has always been the major purpose of traditional class theory to trace and analyse the changes of the class structure'.[3]

Philosophical terms are also sometimes used in drawing the contrast.

As Lenski remarks

'conservatives have tended to be realists with respect to the concept society and nominalists with respect to the concept class, while radicals have generally taken the opposite position'.[4]

That is, conservatives tend to think that society exists independently of any particular exemplification of it in a particular society. They think that society has various needs or functional requisites independent of any that its constituent members in a particular exemplification may have. On the other hand they consider that class is merely a convenient name to give to an aggregate of individuals exhibiting a few common characteristics. It saves us the trouble of repeating that long phrase when we want to talk about them, but beyond a few common characteristics entails nothing further in our conception of them such as, for example, notions of solidarity, class consciousness or interest. Weber is the arch-nominalist in sociology, speaking of classes in terms of probabilities, of the likelihood of individuals acting in a particular way. This and his refusal to consider capitalism, bureaucracy and so on, as anything but ideal types (i.e. concepts we form to obtain an intelligible grasp of some aspect of merely typical probabilities arising out of the interactions of individuals in a particular culture), regularly attracts scornful comment from non-nominalists.[5]

Parsons is sometimes said to be an idealist in contrast to Marx the

[1] J. Rex, *Key Problems of Sociological Theory*. Routledge, London (1963).
[2] Bottomore, op. cit., p. 196.
[3] K. Meyer, 'The Theory of Social Classes', *Transactions of the Second World Congress of Sociology*. London (1954), p. 326.
[4] Lenski, op. cit., p. 23.
[5] For example, G. Gurvitch, *Études sur les classes sociales*. Paris (1966).

materialist. The contrast is instructive as an illustration of how differing conceptions of social structure entail differing conceptions of stratification. For Parsons the central feature of social structure is norms, rules of action regulating relationships among actors in roles. Rules exist in the form of ideas, and behaviour merely exemplifies them. Accordingly, as Lockwood remarks, interests of a non-nominative kind motivated by experience of differential life chances hardly figure in his sociology,[1] while material interests are central to Marx's. For Parsons norms and values have some effective force in shaping social structure, especially the stratification aspect, whereas Marx derived values and norms from social structure, treating them as features of ideology.[2] For him structure in society is to be found in social processes—forms of exchange linking categories. Norms perpetuate a social system, but do not explain it.[3]

The present situation sketched

Few sociologists at the moment think that either pristine Marxism or functionalist theory by itself adequately describes or accounts for all forms of stratification and the phenomena associated with them. Some indication of the kind of criticisms levelled at functionalist theory has been given above. As regards Marxist theory, a representative modern statement regarding its claim to universal applicability is T. B. Bottomore's:

'While (Marxist theory) is highly relevant and useful in analysing social and political conflicts in capitalist societies during a particular period, its utility and relevance elsewhere are much less clear.'[4]

Changes in capitalist society over the last century (see Chapter 5) have produced a situation concerning which many sociologists would agree, to a varying degree, with Dahrendorf's statement that:

'Generally speaking, the Marxist notion of a society split into two antagonistic classes growing out of the property structure of the economy is no longer a correct description of European reality.'[5]

Before outlining the various methodological options open to sociologists

---

[1] D. Lockwood, 'Some Remarks in "The Social System" ', *British Journal of Sociology*, vol. 1, 1956, pp. 134–46.

[2] This contrast (like the preceding) should not be absolutized. Marx recognized that elements of some ideologies have achieved if not universal then qualified validity beyond the societies in which they originated, for example Roman law. On the other hand, Parsons claims that in his analysis 'the old chicken and egg problems about the priorities of ideal and material factors simply lose significance. See T. Parsons, *Societies, Evolutionary and Comparative Perspectives*. Prentice-Hall (1966), p. 115.

[3] See C. Lévi-Strauss, *Structural Anthropology*. N.Y. (1963), p. 281.

[4] Bottomore, op. cit., p. 195.

[5] R. Dahrendorf, 'Recent Changes in the Class Structure of European Societies', *Daedalus*, Winter, 1964, p. 227.

researching into stratification in our own society and describing the
results of current research, I wish to demonstrate, from examples of
pre-industrial stratification (see Chapters 3 and 4) some of the limitations of both theories.

At the same time there are no other general sociological theories of
comparable scope and power. Most contributions to the study of
stratification now take the form of a description of some aspect of it
or the testing of some hypothesis of limited scope, or both. A few
attempts to develop new and more comprehensive approaches to the
subject have not met with unqualified acceptance. The relevance of
J-P. Sartre's remodelling of historical materialism for the analysis of
stratification has yet to be demonstrated.[1] In America G. Lenski[2] has
attempted a synthesis, if not exactly of Marxism and functionalist
theory, at least of radical and conservative approaches. He defines
study of stratification as the study of the distributive process in society,
and the main questions to be answered about any particular society is:
'Who gets what, and why?' His main concepts are power, privilege,
prestige and need. Privilege is having control of some portion of the
surplus of goods and services in society. Control of surplus depends
on power, the probability of a person (or group) being able to carry out
his will even though opposed by others. Production of a surplus requires
a certain level of technological sophistication which some primitive
societies have not attained; accordingly in them distribution is in terms
of need, and equality is the main characteristic of their social systems.
As technology develops inequalities become more pronounced, reaching
their peak in advanced agrarian societies. In industrial society there is
a diminution of the scale of inequality, mainly because of a tremendous
expansion in productivity, because this type of society is so complex
that governors can no longer closely control the distributive process,
and because a democratic ideology prevails. Welcome as Lenski's
attempt is, especially the empirical data he presents and the often
informative generalizations derived from them, his conceptual scheme
is too slight for the grand theme he wishes to develop; the varieties
of equality and inequality are not sufficiently distinguished, for
example. I shall show in the next Chapter that in the simplest societies
privilege is not necessarily distributed in terms of need.

The only general theory comparable in power to functionalism or
Marxism at present being developed is structuralism, which can indeed
be considered as derived from the latter.[3] Structuralists' most impres-

---

[1] J-P. Sartre, *Critique de la Raison Dialectique*. Paris (1960). See also A.
Touraine, *Sociologie de l'Action*. Paris (1965).

[2] Lenski, op. cit.

[3] Lévi-Strauss, op. cit. L. Althusser, *Pour Marx*. Paris (1965). A useful
essay illustrating the derivation is M. Godelier, 'System, Structure and Contradiction in *Das Kapital*', *Structuralism*, ed. M. Lane. Cape, London (1970),
pp. 340–59.

sive achievements lie outside the immediate field of our interest,[1] but one idea which they have developed, that of transformation (used to some extent by Marx) is relevant both to sociological analysis in general and to any attempt at remodelling Marxism. One weakness of the latter is its emphasis on revolution as a necessary final explosion in the process transforming a social structure from one stage to another. In fact there was no revolution finally causing or accompanying the change from ancient to feudal society (see Chapter 3), while the processes which various countries have undergone in changing from feudal to capitalist types have differed markedly, so much so that if the process in France entailed a revolution then the process in England and Japan did not.[2] In transformational analysis one renounces the impossible task of assigning causes to what happened in history; instead, one attempts to render social structures more intelligible by a comparison which retains differences among them. One attempts to show that two or more apparently disparate configurations of categories (i.e. two or more structures) are in fact variations of relations among the same categories. I offer an example of transformational analysis in Chapter 3, pages 63-7.

In the next Chapter I wish to show in a more empirical fashion how different conceptions of social structure entail different conceptions of stratification, and to discuss briefly the question of units of stratification and stratified units. I shall use data from preliterate societies, but wish to stress that the chapter is not intended to give an account of stratification in primitive society, a task that would require the writing of another book.[3]

[1] Lévi-Strauss has argued in his book, *Les Structures Elementaires de la Parente* (Paris, 1949), that the possibility of stratification only emerges with a particular type of kinship system. The thesis is disputed by anthropologists. See, for example, E. Leach, *Lévi-Strauss*. Collins, London (1970), chap. 6.

[2] Barrington Moore, op. cit.

[3] See M. G. Smith, 'Pre-Industrial Stratification Systems', *Social Structure and Mobility in Economic Development*, eds. N. J. Smelser and S. M. Lipset. Routledge, London (1966), pp. 141-76.

Structure and Stratification

ON our conception of social structure depends (*a*) whether or not we consider a particular society to be stratified; (*b*) what we take as the object for study, i.e. the stratified unit; (*c*) what we take as the unit of stratification. By (*c*) I do not mean the unit of systems of stratification which must obviously be the stratum, but the social unit composing the stratum. With regard to (*b*) functionalists are fond of quoting, as evidence for the correctness of their view that there must be a large degree of congruence between the functionally important roles in a society and its system of values, a study by Inkeles and Rossi. In this study the authors compared the ratings or evaluations given to various occupational roles by the members of six relatively industrial modern societies, the USA, the UK, New Zealand, Japan, Germany and Soviet Russia.[1] Their general findings were that

> 'there exists among the six nations a marked degree of agreement on the relative prestige of matched occupations'.

Here they are taking the nation as the stratified unit, and the fact that six, rather than say just two nations, show marked similarities they take as confirming their view. But, are these six nations six societies, or are they six politically independent units within the same society, i.e. relatively industrialized modern society? If the latter, the agreement is hardly surprising. If one conceives of society as Marx did the proper objects for study are the stages in its development. He observed that in his lifetime bourgeois society was spreading its tentacles around the whole world. Modern Marxist analysis sees the five capitalist societies of the six nations listed as, along with others, a sort of super class extracting surplus value from the underdeveloped countries of the world.[2] True, the internal structure of each is still marked by the division into capitalists and proletariat, but conflict between them has been deflected. Capitalist, like proletariat, is now a category of international scope. The segments of the world capitalist ruling class in each bourgeois nation have managed to export their proletariat problem

[1] A. Inkeles and P. H. Rossi, 'National Comparisons of Occupational Prestige', *American Journal of Sociology*, vol. 61, 1956, pp. 329–39.
[2] See P. Baran, *The Political Economy of Growth*. London (1959). Also P. Baran and P. Sweezy, *Monopoly Capital*. N.Y. (1967).

which has now become a problem of foreign policy rather than of home affairs.

Functionalists presumably take the nation state as the stratified unit because their concept of social structure involves the concept of equilibrium in society. The latter concept, in regard at least to more complex societies, implies the existence of clearly defined boundaries to a society and the existence of boundary maintaining mechanisms within it. The nation state is accordingly for them the proper unit for study.

At the same time the authors' findings do point to a problem which Marxist analysis is perhaps not well equipped to deal with. Granted that for Marxists ratings of occupational prestige are not central to their concept of stratification, nevertheless one might have expected, considering that Soviet Russia represents society at another stage of development (or in transition to it), that there would be marked disagreement in the ranking of occupations between it and the others. Moreover, the authors did find some differences in the ranking of a few occupations among the five capitalist nations. As I shall show in the next Chapter political units at the same stage in the Marxian analysis may display marked differences not only as regards values, but also as regards systems of stratification. Clearly Marxian analysis requires supplementation of some sort to account for these differences.

The simplest sort of socio-economic situation which anthropologists encounter is a society whose members live solely by hunting and gathering; the Tiwi of Australia may stand as representative of this situation.[1] Their division of labour is the simplest known; men hunt while women and children gather natural produce, the women's contribution to the food supply being at least equal to the men's. They have no state, not even a tribal council or convocation of any sort. They are divided into nine hunting bands each one hundred to three hundred strong and exploiting about two hundred square miles of territory. Land is vested in the hunting band, its members have exclusive rights to hunt and gather in its territory and to exclude non-members. At the same time, through intermarriage, individuals of different bands are linked to each other by ties of kinship and it is not difficult to change one's band membership. All adults have equal rights to exploit band territory and all possess the requisite weapons and tools.

Kinsfolk cohere into separate households at the core of which is an elderly man, his wives and children. Most have others attached to them, prospective sons-in-law and perhaps visiting cousins. The household is the main unit of production and probably also the main unit of consumption, although most adult males are likely to have obligations

---

[1] C. W. M. Hart and A. R. Pilling, *The Tiwi of Northern Australia*. Holt, Reinhart and Winston, N.Y. (1961). By representative I do not mean that all hunting societies are identical with the Tiwi.

to sometimes give produce to kinsfolk in other households. Though no individuals within the band have exclusive rights of access to and disposal over the means of production, some individuals have exclusive rights to disposal over the means of reproduction. Fathers have exclusive rights of disposal over daughters in marriage, while sons and brothers have rights in the disposal of widows in remarriage. Daughters are betrothed as soon as they are born (sometimes even before they are born), although they do not cohabit with their spouses until after puberty. By giving someone a woman as wife a Tiwi puts the other in his debt, and this debt can only be discharged by either a return gift of a woman or by continual gifts of food. As young men not yet fathers have no daughters, most acquire a wife through the latter process. Thus each household contains prospective sons-in-law contributing by hunting to its food supply, each awaiting the day when his promised bride attains marriageable age and he can set up a household of his own. Established households heads also exchange women amongst themselves, especially widowed sisters. As women are not permitted to remain unmarried and the age gap between a husband and his first wife when they start cohabiting is often about twenty years there is no shortage of supply of the latter.

The aim of an adult Tiwi man is, by the judicious bestowal of women and other gifts, to increase the number of his wives and to build up as large a household as possible. The rewards for success are considerable. First, the larger the household the more likely its members are to produce a surplus of food, thus enabling the head to retire from the daily labour of food production. Second, the larger the household the greater the prestige of its head. Third, the successful head can devote his time to the most valued activities. These are artistic products, such as ceremonial spears or graveposts, or new songs and dances. Spears and graveposts make valuable gifts by which to expand a Tiwi's credit in the continual bargaining with his peers, and by composing new songs and dances he can augment his prestige in the community at large. One respected elderly Tiwi, a 'Carnegie' of the bush, used to make canoes which he donated to the community. Fourth, a Tiwi can spend more time managing his exchange relationships and influencing his peers. Sometimes, for example, a youth attempts to seduce or steal a wife, or flouts an elder's commands. The latter may, if he has enough prestige, persuade his peers to arrange a one sided duel, at which the youth must permit himself to be injured by the offended elder or face several of them armed with spears.

Young men do not form a cohesive group opposed to the elders. They compete with each other for the daughters of the latter. Each has a father, uncles and patrons among them, and each has his own network of exchange relations from which he hopes one day to profit. The pressures mutually exerted by individuals reciprocally obligated, the rights and prestige of influential elders, and magico-religious notions concerning tabooed acts and objects, suffice to maintain an ordered social life. Moreover, the young men are indebted to the old men for the religious knowledge and rights conferred by the process of initiation.

'For females there were no initiation ceremonies but for males it was a long drawn out and elaborate affair, marked by successive stages or grades which began with the status of *Marukumarni*, which a boy entered when he was about fourteen, and did not end finally until he was around twenty-four. Here again we meet the ideology of debt and obligation . . . the obligations contracted in initiation, like obligations contracted at burials or mourning ceremonies, were woven into the kinship and influence systems; indeed the relation of a youth to the men who initiated him was often the beginning of a satellite-patron relationship that lasted half his life.'[1]

A boy has to be initiated in order to acquire the right to marry.

Are we to consider that Tiwi society exemplifies stratification? According to Marxian theory it does not. The unit of ownership of resources is the hunting band, members of which have by birth equal rights of access to them. For stratification to obtain in Marx's sense there would have to be a situation in which a few bands dispossessed the others, depriving individuals in them of access to resources except on condition of handing over a proportion of the fruits of their labour. This simply does not happen, nor does any one band dominate the others politically in any way, nor are they ranked in any prestige order.

Suppose that instead of starting with the unit of ownership of resources, we take the process of accumulation of surplus value and consider how various categories of persons are placed with regard to it. Then old men appear as a category exploiting women and young men. True, but young men become old men, and I do not think it needs any extended argument to conclude that that makes for a very different situation to what Marx had in mind in speaking of class and class conflict. If in our society all men began life as labourers and ended up as millionaire-bishops-artists-judges, and it was an accepted duty of the latter to help the former to replace them we would not consider our society to be yet another instance of a stratified society. When thinking of the latter we have in mind the fact that most labourers remain so for their lifetime, and that most of their sons also become labourers or skilled workmen, certainly not millionaires or bishops, etc. As Ossowski remarks, one of several assumptions which appear to be common to all conceptions of a class society is

[1] C. W. M. Hart and A. R. Pilling, *The Tiwi of Northern Australia*, p. 93.

'that membership of individuals in a social class is relatively permanent'.[1]

This means of course that the question of mobility, especially upwards, is a central one for the assessment as to whether and to what extent we can speak of a society as stratified, as indeed it has become in recent sociology.

There remains the question of whether Tiwi men and women do not form classes in Marx's sense, the women forming a class in itself. If they do it is in a highly qualified sense in that the economic exploitation of one by the other is combined with absolute reproductive interdependence, a relationship that does not obtain between strata in the types of systems of stratification recognized by most sociologists, even though hypergamy[2] is to a certain limited extent practised in most instances. This means that another assumption common to all conceptions of a class society (stratified society) is that a stratum is a self reproducing formation, or rather that it can be, for the extent to which it is or is not will depend on the amount of mobility into and out of it. Yet there are some limiting cases where the assumption does not hold, for example where a slave stratum is recruited mainly from prisoners of war or by slave raids or purchase, or as with the celibate clergy of medieval society, said to form an estate.[3] There is no parallel between these cases and Tiwi sexes; slaves and clergy in these cases are recruited from outside their own ranks, and it does not make sense to say that of Tiwi sexes.[4]

On the other hand, according to functionalists[5] Tiwi society must, like all others, be stratified. Thus roles are differentiated and evaluated in the rank order of old men, young men, and women, with rewards distributed accordingly. Here functionalists distinguish sharply between the individual and the role, and take the role as the unit of stratification. Distribution of rewards among individual men is unequal at any given moment only; individual men go through the same life cycle enjoying

---

[1] S. Ossowski, op. cit., p. 113.

[2] Marriage of a person of lower status to one of a higher.

[3] These cases might also be used to argue that an estate is not necessarily a stratum, provided one rejects Weber's view that stratification occurs in several dimensions, as Barber argues. See B. Barber, *Social Stratification*. N.Y. (1957), pp. 54-7.

[4] In so far as structure in Marx's sense is definable in terms of a process of exchange between categories, which determines forms of superstructure, Tiwi social structure is to be defined in terms of the categories of men between whom exchange of women is permitted. Exchange is not permitted between any two men, if Tiwi conform to the normal Australian type, but only between those who stand in the correct relationship as detailed by their system of kinship and marriage. See, for example, C. Lévi-Strauss, op. cit. Also C. Lévi-Strauss, *Totemism*, tr. R. Needham. Penguin, Harmondsworth (1964).

[5] And some others, see, for example, ed. P. Worsley, *Introducing Sociology*. Penguin, Harmondsworth (1970), p. 285.

equal rewards at the same stages for the most part (see below). There is no inequality if one considers that the individual's career offers a more appropriate temporal span within which to observe the process of distribution of rewards than a tabulation of distributions at a particular moment in time. The functionalists' point is that the roles are permanently unequal. This seems to me to entail an inadequate conception of social structure.[1] We must include in our conception not just a list of roles and of distributions of rewards among them but also the demography of differentiation (e.g. there can only be one king living at any one time), and more important, the processes, rules and institutions regulating individuals' access to roles, for the discontinuities which mark off strata are essentially such processes, institutions and rules.[2] There are no rules or processes which prevent any young Tiwi man from marrying and becoming an old man, in fact all do. Contrast this with the fact that it is impossible for an individual to change his caste membership (although he may leave his caste, see pages 89–90), or the difficulties which a working class person has to overcome in order to become a middle class person (see pages 121–31).

Functionalists might argue that Tiwi society is stratified on other grounds, as follows. Some old men enjoy more prestige than others and accordingly have more influence with their fellows. A few apparently fail altogether in later age, and although respected as old men, bereft of women they become attached to a kinsman's household. However, such an argument takes as the unit of stratification the individual, not the role, and inequalities among individuals occupying the same role is not evidence that they are members of different strata. It is in fact normally the case that within a stratum some individuals enjoy higher prestige, or have more wealth or influence than others.[3] Some functionalists argue, inconsistently, both that all societies are stratified and that, as in our society, the family is universally the unit of stratification. The two propositions cannot both be true of Tiwi society. If it is stratified in the manner functionalists suggest then husbands and wives are in different strata, as are fathers and sons for most of their lives. If among them the family is the unit of stratification then there are no strata, for membership of a successful (high prestige) old man's household confers no special benefits or advantages on young men.[4]

[1] And also to put in question the value of the concept of role for the analysis of microstructures, invaluable as it is for the analysis of microstructures. See S. F. Nadel, *The Theory of Social Structure*. London (1957).

[2] See especially W. Buckley, 'Social Stratification and the Functionalist Theory of Social Differentiation,' *American Sociological Review*, vol. 23, 1958, pp. 369–75.

[3] See J. Littlejohn, *Westrigg*. London (1963), chap. 5. See also chap. 3 below.

[4] The point is forcibly made by Smith, op. cit.

In my view Tiwi society is not stratified, both for the reasons given above, and because to consider it to be so would be to run counter to the two assumptions about the concept of stratum given in the discussion on Marxism and the Tiwi. The worth of a concept of course depends on how much new knowledge or understanding it affords us when applied either in the task of discovering the structure of a particular social system, or in comparing systems. In neither case, it seems to me, does a concept of stratification which includes Tiwi society as an example bring new knowledge nor any understanding.[1]

Finally, regarding the unit of stratification, I think we should leave that to be determined both by the structure of the society studied and by the kind of question to which we seek an answer. In some the lineage and not the family is the unit whose members share a common status.[2] On the other hand, there is sometimes discrimination among members of the same family of a kind relevant to stratification, as when it is the custom among a landowning aristocracy for only the eldest son to succeed to his father's status and inherit his property. There may even be differences between strata in the same society regarding inheritance.[3] For some purposes it may be necessary to use the family or the role as the unit of stratification, for others the individual. In enquiring into individual mobility or into class consciousness, for example, one has to use the individual as the unit, as his role is not mobile, nor is any role conscious of anything.

A note on terminology

The term status is somewhat liberally used in writings both on social structure and social stratification. It is important to distinguish between:

(a) Status meaning position in a social structure, irrespective of considerations of equality and inequality: e.g. my uncle has the status of uncle, and is entitled to treat me as nephew; my fishmonger has the status of fishmonger. The one status is neither higher nor lower than the other, there being no context within which comparison between them in such terms is meaningful.

(b) Status meaning position in a social structure defined by legal immunities or disabilities, e.g. the status of slave, or of freeman.

(c) Status meaning (i) position in a hierarchical organization, e.g. the status of manager; or

(ii) position in a hierarchical scheme which embraces a total

---

[1] I judge that Parsons himself would agree with this. See his *Societies, Evolutionary and Comparative Perspectives*. Prentice-Hall (1966), p. 115.

[2] See Smith, op. cit.

[3] See, for example, E. R. Leach, 'Concepts of Rank and Class among the Kachins of Highland Burma', *Social Inequality*, ed. A. Bétaille. Penguin, Harmondsworth (1969).

society. The term social status is often used for this. It refers not to rights and obligations, but to prestige and the way in which the incumbent of the status is treated by others.

3

Slavery, Ancient and Modern

IF by the term slave society is meant a society in which most production is carried out by slaves, so that it could be said to be dependent on slave labour, then few scholars consider that Athens or Rome were slave societies. Conclusive demonstration one way or the other is impossible for lack of reliable figures on the numbers of slaves in the various occupations. These were agrarian societies, and scholars generally agree that the majority of the population consisted of peasant proprietors and tenants, except in southern Italy and Sicily during certain periods. However, the elite of these societies were landlords whose estates were cultivated, to a considerable but unknown extent, by slaves. It can accordingly be argued that slavery was basic to these societies because slave labour maintained the position of the ruling class.[1] However, the issue is complicated, quite apart from the vagueness of terminology, by a variety of circumstances. For example, the elite also derived much of its wealth from booty and rents, and many of the institutions of state it commanded were maintained by taxes and further, very large numbers of slaves were consumers, not producers.

An objection sometimes raised against the notion that slavery is characteristic of a type of society or stage of social development is that in the early days of modern capitalism slave labour was used in the Americas. This fact certainly qualifies any such notion, although the two forms of slavery differed considerably, reflecting some general differences between ancient and modern society. Even among ancient societies, however, slavery was compatible with a variety of forms of government, republican (both aristocratic and democratic), monarchic, and rule by an emperor and state bureaucracy. This means that we cannot accept both the notion that slavery characterizes a particular type of society and also that, to quote Marx,

'The state and the structure of society are not, from the standpoint of politics, two different things. The state is the structure of society.'[2]

[1] For discussions of the matter see ed. M. I. Finley, *Slavery in Classical Antiquity, Views and Controversies.* Heffer and Sons, Cambridge (1960).
[2] Bottomore and Rubel, *Karl Marx*, Penguin Books, 1963, p. 222.

D

In this chapter I shall outline the position of slaves mainly in Rome, but with occasional reference to Athens, and also sketch in the main features of the system of stratification in Rome. For slavery is usually found in societies markedly stratified in other ways than by the dichotomy of slave and freeman.

The case of Rome is of theoretical interest for a variety of reasons. It illustrates for example the usefulness of the concept of dimensions of stratification and the circumspection with which one must use the dichotomy of ascribed and achieved status. Slavery is presumably an ascribed status,[1] although the two main principles of recruitment into it, capture and birth, are somewhat different. However, precisely because they were ascribed the status, some slaves achieved much more wealth and power than did the majority of citizens.

We have to grasp the meaning of status in the strict legal sense of the term in considering Roman society, the sense that Maine intended when he stated that:

'The movement of progressive societies has hitherto been a movement from status to contract.'[2]

Slavery is sometimes treated as a case of unfree labour, which is a useful enough definition of it in the context of early capitalist society. It is not so useful in the context of ancient society, where slaves were, for example, business men and professors, sculptors and musicians. The slave in ancient society was in a sense the opposite of the citizen in that the slave had no status, while every citizen had the status of citizen. This meant that the slave had no rights within the society of citizens, the *polis* or city state.[3] A slave accordingly was a human being attached to a citizen (or corporation of citizens) in dealings with whom he could not obtain the protection of law. The slave could not initiate legal action, so that in extreme cases his master could kill him with impunity.[4] In banal terms he had to do whatever he was told or risk being beaten or killed. Being a non-citizen meant also that the slave had no political rights. Those two circumstances deprived the slave of freedom as citizens conceived it. Freedom was above all freedom to take part in political activity, military action and public life generally.

---

[1] Though some men *chose* it; see p. 59.

[2] Sir H. S. Maine, *Ancient Law*. World's Classics, OUP (1959), p. 141. By status, Maine meant in this context an ascribed position within a family or lineage. For a useful analysis of the lineage principle in early Rome see F. de Coulanges, *The Ancient City*.

[3] This is especially stressed by H. Lévy Bruhl, *Théorie de l'esclavage*, pp. 151–69. Also in ed. Finley, op. cit.

[4] In imperial Rome this ceased to be the case, to some extent. That is, laws were passed making it an offence to kill a slave. Who would ever hear about an unimportant slave being killed is of course another matter. More important, the meaning of citizenship also changed at this time, see p. 62.

The opposite of this freedom was conceived of as necessity, activity which merely maintained life, production in other words. As production was for the most part production for the household, necessity belonged to the private sphere.[1] Freedom allowed a man to display virtue, especially courage, and win glory; necessity subjected him to obscure and shameful toil. These are formulations of political philosophy, but the attitudes implicit in them are those normal throughout ancient society. A brief sketch of stratification and political organization in republican Rome and democratic Athens illustrates some of the points made above.

The city state was a landowning corporation whose members were descended from parents already citizens. Citizenship in a narrow sense can be regarded as a political-legal status, including rights to vote in public decision-making assemblies and to protection in law, but these were associated in various ways at different periods with tenurial rights and obligations in military service.[2] A major distinction in early republican Rome was that between patricians and plebians, between whom marriage was forbidden by law. The patrician stratum was composed of landowning lineages from whom alone individuals were elected to political office and recruited into the army. Plebians were landless or tenants of the former, did not serve in the army and had no voice in political affairs. They were not full citizens, but neither were they slaves. Some plebian families were perhaps linked with patrician families in patron-client relationships, though probably most clients were themselves less wealthy patricians or strangers settled in Rome as traders.[3] The patron-client tie was an extremely important one throughout Rome's history and political factions in Rome were composed of clients and friends' clients of a few leading lineages. The two parties affirmed the bond by a sacred oath and as well as in general supporting the patron's causes and interests, clients had definite duties, such as to raise the ransom money for a patron captured in war, and the two could not testify against each other in court.

Among the plebians were some labourers or craftsmen free in the sense of being in a position to sell their labour or skills to whomsoever they wished, but there were also large numbers of debt bondsmen. What their position was in early times is not wholly clear. At one period the creditor had the right to sell a defaulting debtor into slavery, though not within the debtor's city state. Let me describe two situations

[1] These and the following sentences are more or less taken from H. Arendt, *The Human Condition*. Chicago (1958). Among other themes the implications of these linked oppositions for ancient culture are brilliantly unfolded.

[2] Weber in particular stresses the connections between citizenship, the right and duty to bear arms, and the rights to land. See M. Weber, 'Agrarverhältnis im Altertum', *Gesammelte-Aufsätze zur Social und Wirtschaftsgeschichte*. Tübingen (1924), pp. 1–288.

[3] See the discussion of this point in ibid.

found among some contemporary West African peoples referred to by this term. (a) A man needs a lump sum of money quickly, for instance, to pay a fine. He offers his services to a rich man in return for a loan and normally labours on his farm. This does not repay the debt but constitutes a sort of interest which has to continue until the original loan is repaid in cash or the master releases the bondsman. The bondsman can of course also work for himself, if he has any time available. (b) A man in need of a lump sum gets a loan by pledging his land as security. He continues to work his land and gives his creditor an agreed amount of the usufruct, often not very much. However, unlike the example given above this debt is heritable, and if not repaid in the debtor's lifetime the creditor is liable to appropriate the land on his death. Another situation combining elements of these two is where parents pledge a child in return for a loan. The child remains a servant in the creditor's household until the debt is repaid.

Reference may also be made here to a situation that sometimes develops in peasant economies where a merchant class arises which has no or few fields for investment except the land of debtors. It has been described in the context of prerevolutionary China by Fei.[1] A peasant proprietor gets a loan from a merchant at a high rate of interest, pleding his land as security. The peasant is still secure in his rights to cultivate the land but the rate of interest, paid in grain, is so high that it is extremely difficult for him ever to repay the loan and he is in effect working for the merchant in return for his own subsistence. Among the merchants a market in titles to pledged land develops, so that the rate of interest tends to keep increasing. The peasants pay this grain interest after harvest when grain is cheap, and may have to buy back grain at exorbitant prices later in the year.

The debt bondsmen in antiquity were in positions analogous to these, or combining elements of these, harsh and unpleasant perhaps, but not those of slaves. Bondsmen still had families and kinsmen able to protect them, within the law, from illegal measures or acts on the part of masters. Slaves on the other hand had no families or kin, did not enjoy legally recognized marriage, or any civil rights. However, the situation of bondsmen was often harsh enough to provoke revolt.

'The debt revolt syndrome', remarks Finley, 'was one of the most significant factors in the early history of both Greece and Rome, and even survived into classical history.'[2]

Another contemporaneous and significant factor, probably connected, was the struggle of the plebians to secure citizenship. This meant the right to serve in the army. There were probably, just before Rome's

[1] H. Fei, *Peasant Life in China*. Routledge, London (1939).
[2] M. I. Finley, 'Between Slavery and Freedom', *Comparative Studies in Society and History*, vol. 6, 1963–4, pp. 233–49.

initial expansion, large numbers of younger sons of small peasant proprietors or tenants without hope of ever acquiring land and probably, as a consequence, without hope of marrying.[1] At any rate Rome's initial expansion was accompanied by the recruitment of plebians into the army, the defeat and expropriation of the land of neighbouring peoples, and the settlement of the victorious veterans on conquered land. As part of the same process the plebians gradually acquired political rights. By 450 BC the prohibition on intermarriage between the strata was repealed and in 326 BC debt bondage of fellow citizens was prohibited, as it had been in Athens two hundred years earlier.[2]

So closely connected were citizenship and army service that the political expression of the plebians' new status took the form of voting in military formation, or a model of it. The summons to service was called *classis*, and because citizens were summonsed in divisions according to the value of the property they owned the term came to be applied to these divisions. Those without land, the *proletarii*, were of course excluded from the divisions and also from armed service. There were seven classes, the first consisting of men who could afford two horses, the appropriate equipment and servants, and who naturally formed the cavalry.[3] Among the six infantry classes the first was approximately ten times richer than the last. For voting purposes in the Assembly each class was divided into centuries, but the number of individuals in these varied systematically from one class to another, so that the knights and the richest infantry class had more centuries than all the others together (see Table One).[4]

TABLE ONE

Class	Wealth (proportional)	Number of centuries per class	
Cavalry	10+	18	98
Infantry 1	10	80	
Infantry 2	7·5—10	20	
Infantry 3	5 — 7·5	20	
Infantry 4	2·5— 5	20	91
Infantry 5	1·1— 2·5	30	
Infantry 6	—1·1	1	

[1] Cf. the age-set tribes of East Africa, such as the Arusha. After a spell of military service, one was entitled to land, a wife, and a voice in the assembly.

[2] M. Rostovtzeff, *Rome*. Galaxy Books, OUP (1960).

[3] At first the *equites* included men of senatorial rank, but later they formed an order or estate separate from the senators.

[4] Adapted from F. R. Cowell, *The Revolutions of Ancient Rome*. Thames and Hudson, London (1962), p. 25. The magistrate in charge of the census by which individuals were allocated to their appropriate class was of course the censor, in this function similar to the Registrar General of Great Britain. However the censor also had the duty of filling vacant places in the Senate, and so was the most powerful magistrate, at least for a certain period.

Each century voted separately and its majority vote was the decision of that century. The final decision of the Assembly was the majority of century votes. Obviously the first two could always outvote the others.

The Assembly in any case had little weight in public affairs compared with the Senate. This was composed of patricians, past magistrates, i.e. holders of public offices such as consul, censor, etc., and senior men of families who had supplied past magistrates, to the number of about three hundred. The Senate conducted Rome's foreign policy, supervised magistrates and generals, and for some generations the Assembly could only vote on decisions referred to it by the Senate. Judges and jurymen were senators or members of senatorial families. As public service was not paid in Rome (unlike Athens) only the rich could put themselves forward for election to public office; success in elections depended on the votes that could be mustered among allies and clients. Public service, however, especially with the expansion of Roman dominion through and beyond Italy, brought its own rewards, booty from wars, slaves, the patronage of lesser office to distribute among clients, and fines and taxes on subject populations. Governorships of conquered provinces were especially lucrative in this last instance.

So far slaves have hardly been mentioned. In the early days of the republic, before the plebians acquired citizenship, slaves were an inconsiderable element in the population, and according to Roman tradition their role was rather that of servant than of chattel.[1] Prisoners of war were either crucified or ransomed, so that most slaves were probably women. At this time children of a master and a slave woman were not themselves necessarily slaves, as they later were.[2] As the plebians gradually acquired the full status of citizen, served in the army instead of cultivating their farms and brought other populations under the dominion of Rome, so the number of slaves increased. Most were prisoners of war though many reached Rome via one of the slave markets such as Delos, where it is said that ten thousand slaves per day were regularly sold.

Some of Rome's neighbouring allies who fought in the wars against Carthage and in the East also acquired Roman citizenship. As more people entered and consolidated their positions as citizens of Rome, the more slaves increased in the polity. Free and unfree populations increased simultaneously. As non-citizens slaves naturally had no part in Senate or Assembly proceedings and could not hold political office or bear arms. They were extensively used in the navy, but that was a disgraceful service in the eyes of the soldier citizens. As Rome expanded,

[1] C. W. Westrup, *The Roman Slave in Early Times*. Copenhagen (1956).
[2] K. Hopkins, 'Slavery in Classical Antiquity', *Caste and Race*, eds. A. Reuck and J. Knight. Churchill, London (1967), pp. 166–78.

the amount of land at the disposal of the Senate increased enormously. This was leased out to citizens, but naturally the richer citizens, senators and knights (the generals, governors and officials who profited most from war), acquired most of the leases, and they had the money to purchase slaves to work the huge estates made available in this way. On their extensive *latifundia* they produced wines, oil and hides for the market, and corn for the state granaries in Rome, from which it was either sold at cheap rates or distributed free to citizens (from 123 BC). The increase in the slave population of the republic is associated with expanding dominion, almost continuous warfare, increase in the scope of market economy and the use of money in transactions, absence of Roman farmer citizens on military expeditions abroad, and with the extension of citizenship to categories who had hitherto not enjoyed the status.

Of Roman citizens one could say, in modern sociological terms, that among them there was a high degree of status consistency. Political and economic positions were coterminous; new rich men were admitted to senatorial rank although the prestige of ancient lineage remained a great advantage in the competition for public office. The extent to which a citizen could actually obtain protection in law, as distinct from the theoretical equality of citizens, was probably correlated with his position in these other two dimensions. Legal protection depended to some extent on the citizen's patron who would no doubt estimate his worth, financial or otherwise, before deciding how far to extend his patronage.

Athenian democracy, where the patron-client relation was never important, was different. All adult male citizens had equal political and legal rights and opportunities. All were members of the Assembly, a sovereign body which elected generals and financial officers and which met regularly both to formulate policy and to decide on detailed issues of finance, foreign affairs and so on. Its administrative cadre was a Council of five hundred chosen annually by lot from the city wards in proportion to their size. The Council supervised magistrates and acted as a steering committee for the Assembly. The president of both bodies was chosen daily by lot. Juries, empanelled by lot from a body of 6,000 citizens chosen annually by lot, decided not only private cases but public charges such as treason or peculation. In order that the poorer could afford the time for public service, citizens on duty (from the time of Pericles) were paid while performing it.[1] A few property classes were recognized but, it seems, only for the purpose of graded taxation and liability for armed service, the poorer being liable for service in the navy. The prestige of ancient noble lineage and of present wealth were always an advantage in seeking election

[1] A. H. M. Jones, 'The Economic Basis of Athenian Democracy', *Past and Present*, no. 1, Feb. 1952, pp. 13–31.

to public office, but all citizens were entitled to nomination (unless disqualified by delicts of various sorts).[1] It is difficult to imagine more democratic arrangements. Yet there were vast differences in wealth among citizens and sharply distinguished from them, by absence of political and legal rights, were the slaves.[2]

Reliable figures are lacking for the size of the slave populations of these times. Finley[3] suggests for Athens of the fourth and fifth centuries eighty thousand to one hundred thousand, averaging three to four slaves per free household, while Jones suggests a figure of twenty thousand or one per adult citizen.[4] Some citizens of course had no slaves while a few had several thousands each. However, Athens was a trade and craft centre and it is probable that at all times in the countryside, both in Athens and in Rome, the majority of those engaged in agriculture were self employed peasants, except in southern Italy and Sicily at certain periods.

We are accustomed to think of slavery in its modern forms as exemplified in the plantation slavery of the West Indies and the American South. On each plantation were masses of servile negro labourers exposed to the brutality of a few white overseers, with a very small proportion in slightly privileged positions as craftsmen or domestic servants. By 1795 there were in Jamaica 291,000 slaves, the vast majority plantation labourers, to about 17,000 resident whites.[5] Above all we think of a repressive social system, of masters discouraging slaves from buying their freedom, and the slave seeing little point in it anyway, as a free negro was no better off. Despised, distrusted and thrown into a backwater in a market economy, his chances of starving to death were probably greater as a freed man than as a slave.[6] We have to revise our conception of slavery somewhat in considering its manifestations in ancient society, especially Athens where, for example, the police force was composed of slaves.[7]

Slaves in ancient society engaged in all occupations except political and military, while there were no occupations slaves followed in which freemen (citizens) were not to be found. In Athens most bank managers were slaves, as were clerks in public audit departments. Many were shopkeepers, craftsmen and business agents. Large numbers were domestic servants[8] and slaves probably predominated in mining and

---

[1] A. Andrews, *The Greeks*. Weidenfeld and Nicolson, London (1967).

[2] E. Barker, *Greek Political Theory*. Methuen, London (1964).

[3] M. I. Finley, 'Was Greek Civilization Based on Slave Labour ?', ed. Finley, op. cit.

[4] A. H. M. Jones, 'Slavery in the Ancient World', in ed. Finley, ibid.

[5] O. Patterson, *The Sociology of Slavery*. London (1967).

[6] Ibid.

[7] On the attitude to slaves in Athens see D. H. F. Kitto, *The Greeks*. Penguin, Harmondsworth (1951).

[8] Some of these were perhaps in engaged in craft work such as weaving.

quarrying. Craftsmen and commercial slaves were usually not closely supervised, but had to bring their master a fixed proportion of their earnings (the literal meaning of one Greek word used of slaves is simply 'pay bringer'). The miners, numbering at one time about thirty thousand, were probably subject to the dreadful conditions and brutal treatment we think of as typical of slavery, but some citizens were also miners, at least for a period in their lives.

In Rome slaves were also found in all the occupations mentioned.[1] For a long time the Rome fire brigade, seven thousand strong, was manned by slaves, as was the navy including in many cases ships' captains. Direct dealings in trade and commerce were regarded as disgraceful pursuits for the upper class citizens and indeed were prohibited to senators, for whom landowning, war and administration were the proper sources of income. A great deal of trade and commerce was conducted by slaves and freedmen, as well as by foreigners in the position of client. But the upper classes also profited from it, through the institution of the *peculium*, a sum of money or property (a ship, craft shop, etc.) given to a slave to manage, the profits being divided between master and slave as the master decided. Some slaves became very rich in this way, investing their gains in the business they managed or elsewhere, often in slave trading. Such a slave could make contracts, although laws regarding liability varied at different periods. Rich slaves owned slaves of their own, and often on manumission the freed slave received the *peculium* as a parting gift from his ex-master. It follows that slaves (and freedmen) were to be found at many economic levels, and some were richer and some more secure than many poor citizens. Craft industry, for example, was mostly administered and owned by municipalities. The slaves in them, examples of whose work we admire in our museums, enjoyed a secure if modest living at the same wage rates as free craftsmen. As Barrow points out, one may infer from some laws prohibiting citizens from passing themselves off as slaves that some citizens preferred to live as slaves.[2]

Manumission of slaves was common, especially during late republican and early empire periods. At different periods freedmen suffered various liabilities distinguishing them from citizens: they could not vote for example, or under certain conditions a freedman's property on death reverted to his ex-master, and he was bound by custom to become a client of his ex-master. Augustus created three classes of freedman one of which, composed of those who had been especially fractious as slaves, was prohibited from making wills or living within one hundred miles of Rome. Of vastly greater significance is that when Augustus

[1] See R. H. Barrow, *Slavery in the Roman Empire*. Methuen, London (1929).
[2] Ibid.

took command of the Roman polity, depriving the status of citizen of its political content, his private slave secretaries became virtual ministers of state, administering the treasury in particular. It was some generations before men at the level of the knight class accepted office in the imperial administration. Meanwhile the emperor's secretariat, slaves and freedmen, enjoyed more authority than did senators and at times presided over the destiny of the empire, as when in AD 49 the freedman Narcissus foiled a plot to kill and supplant the Emperor Claudius. He persuaded the Emperor to give him command of the guard for a day, during which he had Claudius' wife, chief conspirator along with G. Silius, assassinated. In imperial Rome a slave's authority and economic position depended on what general category of slave he belonged to, state (i.e. emperor's household), municipal or private, on his occupation, on the wealth of his master, and on his own ability as an administrator or manager of a *peculium*.

This kind of situation has been reported of many pre-industrial slave-employing societies where ultimate power and authority is in the hands of a king or emperor, for example the Nupe empire in Nigeria.[1] There, slaves as well as kinsmen of the reigning monarch were appointed to many of the highest offices, even army commands. Slave officials enjoyed the confidence of their master rather more than did his kinsmen. The latter and other upper class grandees were liable to use the authority and power of high office against him, while slaves, being utterly dependent on him, would not and at the same time would, on their master's behalf, monitor the activities of non-slave office holders. Of course not all royal slaves attained high office by any means, but all attached to the court in a non-menial position could compete for it. We should note that in these societies generally, and certainly in Rome, race was irrelevant to the question of who could be enslaved, for slaves were of all races.

It is not clear what social status means in a society such as Rome: the extent to which a man resembles in deed some mythical or legendary figure perhaps. In so far as we can speak of it, slaves were sensitive about the social status of their masters. Jones cites an illuminating case of four lecturers:

> 'Those who had a house laboured under a heavy mortgage, others lived in lodgings "like cobblers". They could barely afford to marry, and congratulated themselves if they had only one child. They owed money to the baker, and had to sell their wives' trinkets to meet the bill. These unfortunates could afford only three slaves, or even two, who were insolent to their masters because they had not many fellow servants.'[2]

---

[1] S. F. Nadel, *A Black Byzantium*. OUP (1942).
[2] Jones, 'Slavery in the Ancient World', ed. Finley, op. cit., p. 1.

Treatment of slaves varied a great deal according to their occupations, and also between societies according to differences in ethos[1] between them. Unskilled labourers on plantations or in mines were expendable and probably suffered a great deal.[2] In Rome slave witnesses were liable to torture but magistrates differed in their readiness to use it and in their estimate of the reliability of evidence obtained in this way. Roman slaves were admitted into many cults and formed burial and savings clubs, and often in this way helped each other to buy freedom. Spartans, who sometimes had to deal with rebellions among their helots,[3] sneered that slaves were indistinguishable from citizens in the streets of Athens, where the slaves never rebelled. More boisterous in temperament perhaps than the Greeks, or perhaps like Marx keenly aware of the physiological infrastructure to life and unlike Marx fascinated[4] by the spectacle of its most disastrous intrusion into personal existence, Romans conscripted numbers of slaves into the entertainment industry. Some of these however, in imperial times, were citizens who had been convicted of capital crimes, army deserters, traitors, murderers and dangerous psychopaths. Moreover during the later days of the Republic

'freedom had so fallen in value that freemen often sold themselves for board and wages as gladiatorial slaves'.[5]

The circus was never popular with Greeks, who much preferred athletic contests. Finally, if Romans were sometimes merciless in their treatment of slaves they were equally so at times in their treatment of each other, particularly during the period of civil wars (90 BC to 27 BC). By one estimate Marius liquidated fifty senators and one thousand knights, Sulla forty senators and one thousand six hundred knights, not in battle but in proscriptions afterwards.[6]

'The sight of headless bodies thrown out on the streets and trampled underfoot excited not so much pity as a general fear and trembling.'[7]

Plutarch describes instances of slaves risking their own lives to save their master's during these blood-baths.

Slave rebellions and revolutions

If we take revolution to mean an organized violent attack on a polity by a section of its population which results in a considerable change in its social structure, there were no slave revolutions in ancient

[1] In the sense of ethos as used by G. Bateson, *Naven*. Cambridge (1936).
[2] This is by no means certain.
[3] Helots were not exactly slaves, but not citizens either.
[4] The fascination is described by Saint Augustine, *Confessions*. Penguin, Harmondsworth (1970).
[5] T. Mommsen, *History of Rome*. Owen, London (1960), p. 503.
[6] Cowell, op. cit., p. 127.   [7] Plutarch, *Life of Marius*.

society. The debt bondsmen who revolted or rioted from time to time did so not with the intention of abolishing slavery or even necessarily the institution of debt bondage. They wanted to extricate themselves from their own intolerable situation. There were never any slave rebellions in Athens, and only for a short period between 140 BC and 70 BC were they frequent in Roman dominions. They were all suppressed with great violence. The slaves' aim was never to establish a new social order without slavery but to escape from their own position, which some did by making their way back to their own country or by becoming bandits or pirates. Where occasionally they were temporarily successful in driving off their Roman masters and setting up some social order they merely replicated an existing one as in Sicily, where they enslaved those who opposed them. Their leader took the title of King Antiochus and established a court modelled on those of other east Mediterranean monarchs.[1]

Probably the most historically famous of the slave revolts was the last, led by the gladiator Spartacus and his companions. For a few years, with an army of fugitives over a hundred thousand strong, they terrorized southern Italy and defeated several Roman armies. However, men defected to form separate bandit gangs, and after the last battle the six thousand of his men who survived to be taken prisoner were crucified along the road between Rome and Capua. Crucifixion at that time, and afterwards, probably meant being impaled through the anus on a spike or spear. There was no further organized defiance on the part of slaves until many centuries later when the empire had in any case begun to disintegrate.[2] Talcott Parson's idea that power enters into systems of stratification merely as a factor that disturbs perfect integration in terms of values and associated ranking of roles or other social units is not applicable to Rome. Power, in the sense of command of organized violence as the means to actualize interests, not only maintained the system of stratification but was what the system was intended to provide for its upper stratum. Power at that time meant having command over armed men, not authority to use tricky machines like H-bombs. Increasing numbers of slaves helped to expand the number of enfranchised peasants and with the larger citizen army so made available the patricians conquered the Mediterranean world. Marx's notion that the state is the structure of society is more nearly applicable to Rome than to any other society.[3] The case of Rome, where no-one

[1] P. Green, 'The First Sicilian Slave War,' Past and Present, no. 20, November 1961, pp. 10–29.

[2] E. P. Thompson, 'Peasant Revolts in Late Roman Gaul and Spain', Past and Present, no. 2, November 1952.

[3] H. Arendt writes: 'Marx's model of explanation was the ancient institution of slavery, where clearly a ruling class, as he was to call it, had possessed itself of the means with which to force a subject class to bear life's toil and burden for it'. H. Arendt, On Revolution. Faber and Faber, London (1963), p. 57.

ever revolted against the institution of slavery, although slaves sometimes rebelled against being slaves, would seem to put in question the
functionalist view that society is integrated through consensus on
values. There was consensus on values, but it was violence that maintained the structure.

The relative infrequency of organized rebellion does not mean that
slaves readily accepted their position. Although they never revolted
they frequently took the opportunity provided by war to flee from
Athens, and fugitive slaves were commonplace in Roman dominions.
The army or the navy frequently had to deal with bandits and pirates
many of whom were runaway slaves. It is in any case difficult for slaves
to organize, or to procure arms if they do. Two recent studies indicate
the conditions in which slaves are most likely to organize rebellion
with some measure of success. These are where slaves far outnumber
the non-slave population, and where the slave population includes a
fair proportion of men who were of high status in their own society
before being enslaved. Both conditions obtained for a while in Roman
Sicily[1] and in British Jamaica, and in the latter a sucessful negro revolt
led to the establishment of a small but sovereign negro polity in one
corner of the island.[2] However, it was left in peace largely because its
leaders agreed to help the British recapture other runaway slaves.
Perhaps the only completely successful slave rebellion in history has
been that in Haitii led by Toussiant L'Ouverture.

The slave rebellions in classical times in no way altered the social
structure. It is in any case wrong to think of revolutions as violent
outbreaks by only the lower oppressed strata of society. Many successful ones are the work of upper classes, or sections of them. Rome's
most successful revolution, the change from a republic to a principate,
was carried through by a few patricians, particularly Caesar and his
heir Augustus.[3] With the establishment and consolidation of the
empire Roman society changed considerably, and with it the position
of slaves and the organization of labour in general.

We have to think of the economy of Rome as operating on three
places involving different units and classes of people and entailing
different kinds of relations. (a) There was a self subsistent peasantry,
and self sufficient landlord estates. (b) There was some production
for the market, both a local market and for export. Most of this was
produced by slaves. Exports were mainly luxury goods consumed by
town patriciates in the Mediterranean ports and in Rome itself; the
volume of this export trade was very small by modern standards.

[1] Green, *The First Sicilian Slave War*, op. cit.
[2] Patterson, op. cit.
[3] Those who supported Caesar were mostly of non-senatorial rank, but also
non-slaves. One might perhaps call it a middle class revolution with an upper
class leader, if only the term class were not so inappropriate.

(c) There was redistribution of several sorts. Taxes on citizens and subject populations paid for public works, circuses and state projects generally. Landlords and patrons extracted some of the peasants' production in the form of rents and gifts. A major portion of the wealth which flowed to Rome however consisted of war booty and exactions from provincial peoples. Soldiers kept what booty they could, and generals such as Pompey and Caesar amassed huge fortunes from it. The rich disbursed a great deal of wealth in maintaining luxurious establishments in various parts of the empire and sumptuous palaces in Rome. A rich man would have from four thousand to ten thousand household slaves, some of them secretaries and tutors, but the majority were simply servants organized in a ridiculously elaborate division of labour.[1] The slave population in republican times may well have been subsidised by booty.[2]

As Marx pointed out, the Greeks and Romans had no theory of economic value, no political economy, only enquiry

'about what kind of property creates the best citizens'.[3]

However, one does not have to have a theory of value to appreciate the consequences of the law of diminishing returns in personal economic projects,[4] and already in Cicero's day landlords were finding it more profitable in some circumstances to farm through *coloni* rather than slaves,[5] i.e. through forms of tenure whereby the landlord was entitled to a proportion of the labour or production of his peasant tenants.

With the consolidation of the empire the emphasis in redistribution changed from booty to tax collecting and a vast bureaucracy, mostly of slaves, was developed to administer and execute fiscal programmes. The boundaries of the empire were fixed, wars became defensive, and a professional army was created drawing peasant recruits from almost everywhere within the empire. Almost everyone became a citizen (AD 213), equally liable to tax and the jurisdiction of the emperor, although old distinctions remained in the form of ranked titles and differential legal immunities. The main distinction was between *honestiores* and *humiliores*. The former were those of senatorial and knightly rank along with soldiers of various grades and those who had

---

[1] For details see J. Carcopino, *Daily Life in Ancient Rome*. Routledge, London (1941).

[2] Hopkins, op. cit.

[3] Marx, *Pre-Capitalist Economic Formations*, ed. Hobsbawm. Lawrence and Wishart, London (1964), p. 84.

[4] As R. Firth demonstrates in *Primitive Polynesian Economy*. Routledge, London (1939).

[5] The position of the *coloni* varied at different periods; sometimes they were tied to the land and sometimes not. See, for example, T. Frank, *A History of Rome*. Cape, London (undated).

held municipal office in provincial towns, and the latter were simply the rest. For the same type of delict the former were punished only by banishment to some provincial outpost, or at most confiscation of property, while the latter were sent to the mines or the amphitheatre, or crucified.

The supply of slaves by capture diminished, the proportion of slaves in the agricultural population decreased, and most slaves were so by birth. At the same time taxes on towns, to supply transport, etc., for the army, adversely affected trade, and the whole weight of imperial administration began to bear on inland agricultural populations whose production was now the main source of wealth. Estate owners and managers were made responsible for submitting the tax from their free peasantry. Their solution to the problems posed them by these developments was to institute new forms of tenure. As a particular incentive to production they restored marriage and the family to slaves while at the same time putting on them the responsibility for the maintenance of their families by granting them rights to the use of land.[1] But many free peasants already held land in return for labour services, or rents in kind, or both, and the distinction between free and unfree ceased to have the sharp meaning it once had. Finally, to prevent free peasants evading tax by moving just before payment was due, laws were passed prohibiting movement, thus tying most peasant cultivators to particular estates. These arrangements were close to feudal forms of organization, and as Weber points out the restoration to slaves of marriage and the family accompanied, or was accompanied by, growing acceptance of Christianity.

Ancient and modern slavery

Certain economic and technological conditions favour the institution of slavery as a method of using or exploiting labour. These are where land is cheap and plentiful and there is an assured market for crops which can be raised by highly routine procedures requiring little skill but intensive application of labour.[2] These conditions obtained in various parts of Roman territory and in America. Both ancient and modern slavery can be regarded as a response to favourable conditions during a period of expansion when labour was in short supply. In both periods the upper classes had little regard for the sufferings of the lower classes. If African slaves were brutally treated, the sailors who brought them to America were hardly less so. Some were as

---

[1] M. Weber, 'Die Sozialen Gründe des Untergangs der Antiken Kultur', *Gesammelte Aufsätze zur Social-und Wirtschaftsgeschichte*, op. cit., pp. 189–311. M. Bloch, 'Comment et Pourquoi Finit l'esclavage Antique', ed. Finley, op. cit.

[2] E. Williams, *Capitalism and Slavery*. André Deutsch, London (1964).

much slaves by capture, in the back streets of British seaports, as the Romans' war prisoners. Women and children in British mines at the time might well have benefited in health from a few months' holiday labouring on an upland Jamaican plantation.

Yet the similarities in general conditions only emphasize the differences between ancient and modern slavery. They stand in an inverse and opposite relation with regard to the two realms, social organization and economic activity. Rome was a society organized in terms of status (strict sense) ascribed in the first instance by birth. However, it had to accommodate itself to expanding economic activity, to the fact that trade and capitalistic production as well as war create wealth, and that if status implies the right to command the actions of others wealth does so regardless of rights. All this was recognized and new wealthy men were admitted to senatorial and knightly rank. Yet trade, industry and commerce remained disgraceful. However, being by status always in absolute authority over them, the Romans could allow slaves to produce anything, and they would benefit from it.

Eighteenth-century Britain and America represent society shaped to the requirements of a market economy, in its leading principles a society of property holders and free labourers. Status had practically disappeared, all were equally subjects of the state.[1] Yet this free society of 'equals in the eyes of the law' had not yet freed itself from the attitudes appropriate to the recent feudal past, when society was organized in terms of status and rank. Both in the West Indies and the American South property owners sought to re-establish a society based on hereditary status, with themselves as the aristocrats. Being by property-owing richer, but in status no different from anyone else, they had to suppress their labouring class without the aid of law,[2] hence the discouragement of freedom buying, or local economic development and of a division of labour which would have made freedom worth seeking, but which would also have created gradations of wealth. As wealth was their only source of status, now become mere social status, this would have compromised the sharp and absolute distinction between themselves and the labourers which they wanted to establish. They went so far indeed as to compromise the local

---

[1] If not in every detail, at least that was the aim of political and legal reform at the time.

[2] This may seem a sweeping statement. However, according to Patterson, op. cit., there never was a law of slavery in the British West Indies. In the American South laws were indeed framed depriving negoes of some of the normal rights of citizens, e.g. prohibiting them from marrying white women. Yet, (i) these laws varied greatly from one state to another, while negroes were equally suppressed everywhere; the inference that law was irrelevant to the definition of who a person was would seem to be confirmed by, (ii) the abolition of slavery made no difference to the position of negroes, or only gradually and to a limited extent.

symbols by which they sought to display their aristocratic position. Their mansions, pretentious in style, used to fall down often because they were so badly built.[1]

Intensive exploitation of slaves whether by gang labour or the *peculium* was characteristic of the 'heartlands'[2] of the empire and of Rome itself. Slavery in anglo-saxon America was characteristic of the periphery. It was in fact illegal in Britain and the abolition movement originated there. In America it was abolished by military action initiated by the industrial, democratic North against the rural, aristocratic South, the historically victorious centre against the historically doomed periphery.

In their excesses the two systems display the same relation to each other. In Rome large numbers of slaves were consumers and the division of labour there reached its apogee in service distinctions. Really conspicuous consumption however, consisted in freeing large numbers of slaves. Competition among the rich in this way attained such heights that the emperor, in the interest of social order, had to pass laws forbidding the manumission by the owner of more than one-fifth of his slaves at a time.[3] Yet in Rome a slave could be killed just as easily as he might be freed, and some masters became notorious for entertainments in the course of which a few slaves were murdered. Either way the owner attained a temporary rise into the highest status by becoming, for the slave, fate. Romans often imitated the gods, from whom indeed some patricians could trace descent. On platforms in their gardens and parks, appropriately costumed and garlanded, they ate and drank to music sung by some local Orpheus while deer and wild boar, specially trained by their slave psychologists, emerged from the shrubbery to gather round. In the modern society conspicuous consumption could also take the form of lavish feasting and house building. Often the competitor ruined himself and his creditors,[4] and even if successful, merely succeeded in turning culture into a stratagem in business enterprise. At any rate, the gods being dead and Jehovah both remote and inimitable, the utmost distance that could be established between one man and another could only be that between the absolute subject and the absolute object, but the cruelty masters sometimes practised on slaves to establish the distance has merely branded them as psychological cripples.[5]

Slavery was an institution long before the Romans had any theory about it. When they did theorize about it they saw it in terms of

[1] In the West Indies at any rate.
[2] Hopkins, op. cit.
[3] Barrow, op. cit.
[4] L. Stone, 'Social Mobility in England', *Past and Present*, no. 33, April 1966, pp. 16–55.
[5] On this topic see J. P. Sartre, *L'Etre et le Neant*. Paris (1948).

E

status, not in terms of natural differences. People of all races were slaves. As their jurist Florentinus put it,

> 'slavery is an institution of the *ius gentium* whereby someone is subject to the dominion of another, contrary to nature'.[1]

In production accordingly slaves could be the same as citizens, because not citizens. Men were different by status. For the moderns, men are the same by status, but different by social status, i.e. levels of consumpton and style of life. To prevent negroes from becoming the same as or even comparable to their masters in consumption they had to be different in production. They stayed as unskilled labour, it was maintained, because that was all they were capable of. Men were decreed to be different by nature.[2]

The induction of slave personnel into Roman society and their exclusion from modern society is again instructive. Political rivalry among the great men of Rome combined with the vast estates and clientele they had to manage led to the growth of a huge class of expert slave administrators who alone, being utterly dependent on them, could be entrusted with their masters' interests. These slaves, highly educated, secure and well fed, learned the secrets of administration and state-craft while the majority of citizens played the part of angry mobs or marched into battle. When Augustus became emperor nothing was more inevitable than that slaves should run his empire. In America economic competition among capitalists turned the slave areas into backwaters, where the opportunities for the unskilled ever to learn the skills requisite for better jobs in an industrial society continually decreased. By the middle of the twentieth century it was probably true, as racists proclaimed, that the majority of adult negroes in these areas were fit for nothing but labour.

A comparison of slavery in anglo-saxon and in Iberian America would be instructive in the light of these remarks. Slavery in South America was more like Roman slavery in many ways. The whole Iberian project there was directed and controlled by King and Church to a far greater extent; slaves were less 'different by nature' and more 'different by status'; slaves were encouraged to buy their freedom and enter the crafts, and gradations of status were recognized.[3] A *latifundia*

---

[1] Quoted in Finley, op. cit., p. 36. There is not space here for discussion as to what the Romans meant by nature, or by the law of nature. Some essential reading is Plato, *Protagorus*. Penguin, Harmondsworth (1970). Maine, op. cit. L. Strauss, *Natural Right and History*. Chicago (1953).

[2] A somewhat different but related argument is put forward in a discussion of caste, racism and social stratification by L. Dumont, *Contributions to Indian Sociology*, no. 5, pp. 20–43.

[3] See S. M. Elkins, 'Slavery and its Aftermath in the Western Hemisphere', eds. Reuck and Knight, op. cit., pp. 192–203.

economy was developed and politics was organized through patron-client relations. The problems bequeathed each society from the slave episode are characteristically different. Iberian America finds it difficult to modernize, i.e. to develop industry and political democracy, while America and Britain have the problem of race relations.

4

Caste Society

THE Hindu caste system[1] is of special interest to the student of stratification. Largely because of its close connections with the Hindu
religion and because Indian village economy is not a market economy
scholars disagree as to its nature and functions. Some treat it as a
division of labour similar in principle to European feudal systems but
in which landowners to an excessive degree exploit the landless, aided
in this by a religion peculiarly successful in diverting the exploited
from arriving at a consciousness of their true situation. Others treat it
as primarily a liturgical or religious organization serving ends distinct
from, though inevitably involved in, economic ones. Many try to find
some middle ground for interpretation or simply attempt to answer
specific questions about particular aspects of the system. Another
related controversy concerns the question as to whether or not the
system is specific to India (understood in the first instance as Hindu
India), or to what extent we can speak of caste as an element in many
systems of stratification, present in varying degree or form. The view
that the term can be usefully applied in societies outside India is
implicit in our incorporation of the word into ordinary English usage,
as when we say, for example, that Junkers formed a military caste
which ruled Germany.

If we are to think about caste without prejudging the issue we must
recognize that the term is not an Indian one and that we need several
terms to distinguish various kinds of collectivities or units to which the
term caste has been applied. The word is an English rendering of the
Portuguese *casta* meaning race, lineage or pure stock. This in turn is
derived from the Latin *castus* which has a range of meanings from
morally pure, disinterested, to unpolluted. Indians have a variety of
terms for referring to units in their social system, the two main ones
being *varna* and *jati*.

In early Vedic texts Hindu society is described as composed of four
estates, groups having different social functions and ranked in order
of worth or social honour. These, the varna, are in rank order: first
the Brahmins, priests who have the sole right to perform the act of

---

[1] The most magisterial survey of the system is by L. Dumont, *Homo
Hierarchicus*. Gallimard, Paris (1966). This work, which abounds in references,
is essential reading for those who wish to understand the caste system.

sacrifice on others' behalf; second the Kshatriya, kings and warriors; third the Vaisya, who herd cattle; the fourth and last estate is the Sudra, menials and labourers whose duty is to serve the other three. Indians still use this model in conceptualizing their social system. In this account of Indian society the untouchables are passed over in silence, but are understood to be below the Sudra in rank. These strata (the description goes) are endogamous, and as the individual may not become a member of any other than the one he was born into, each forms a closed group, self recruiting and impermeable. They also differ markedly in customs and culture, e.g. Brahmins prohibit widow remarriage but the others do not; and the top three are distinguished from the others as twice born, meaning that they are entitled to pass through a ceremony which confers upon them a spiritual rebirth whereby they inhabit the spiritual realm on a higher plane than the others.

The varna model is still relevant in Indian thought but in modern times another somewhat different one is sometimes used by Indians

CHART ONE

Approximate hierarchy of caste groups in Bisipara[1]

A	High Hindus	1	Brahmin
		2	Warrior
		3	Herdsman or Distillier or Writer or Oriya
		4	Fisherman
		5*	Kond potter
		6*	Kond or Kond herdsman
		7*	Christian
		8*	Muslim
B	Low Hindus	1	Templeman
		2	Barber
		3	Washerman
		4	Weaver
		Line of pollution	
C	Untouchables	1	Outcaste
		2	Basketmaker
		3	Sweeper

Note: (1) The word 'or' indicates that caste groups under this number dispute for precedence.

(2) Caste groups marked with an asterisk are those considered non-Hindu. However, informants could allot them a place in a table of precedence. In the case of converts to Christianity and Islam, their rank depends on the caste of their pagan ancestors. Converted outcastes, for instance, are still untouchable.

[1] From F. C. Bailey, *Caste and the Economic Frontier.* Manchester (1957). p. 8.

and often by foreign scholars. This is a division of the population into three ranked categories, respectively Brahmins, clean non-Brahmins and unclean non-Brahmins. Here is an example of the scheme as applied to a particular village population. Each category is further subdivided into smaller units normally called jati (Chart One).

This threefold scheme is of interest mainly because it stresses, instead of social function, the basic principle of caste society, i.e. a purity-impurity polarity in terms of which castes are ranked. As to the term caste, it is applied in English writings on the subject to a variety of units, sometimes to the varna, and sometimes to categories of persons bearing (within a given linguistic region) a common caste name, often of an occupation they are traditionally associated with; of these Hutton remarks that

'to say that there are some three thousand different castes in India is probably to run little risk of exaggeration'.[1]

The term is also applied to smaller segments within these categories, sometimes called subcastes, and also to those locally defined units called jati. A jati comprises a' number of lineages,[2] each comprising usually a number of households, who live in the same village or group of villages

'practising a traditional occupation and enjoying a certain amount of cultural, ritual and jurisdictional autonomy'.[3]

Between jati there are restrictions on intermarriages, on commensality and invarying degree on other forms of social intercourse.

Consider first the purity-impurity polarity by reference to which castes are ranked, the Brahmins representing a condition of purity[4] and the untouchables of impurity. Among the more highly educated, purity and impurity are linked with the conception of the soul in an elaborate theology. However, for both high and low the major sources of impurity are the same. These are death, excretions from the human body, exuviae both human (e.g. hair) and animal (hides, etc.), and contact with unclean animals such as the pig. The occupations of untouchables and of some castes in the clean category bring them into more or less permanent contact with these substances. Thus the sweeper's task is to remove faeces from household latrines, the washer-man's to clean soiled clothes. Swineherds are impure because pigs defile. Normally an untouchable caste disposes of the carcases of beasts.

[1] J. H. Hutton, *Caste in India*. OUP (1946), p. 128.
[2] A lineage is a number of genealogically linked people claiming descent from a common ancestor or ancestress.
[3] S. M. Srinivas, *Religion and Society among the Coorgs of India*. OUP (1952), p. 24.
[4] For a modern treatment of this subject see M. Douglas, *Purity and Danger*. Routledge, London (1966).

Brahmins, the priests and scholars, are of course forbidden these and other defiling occupations. Caste occupations, or at least those which determine caste level in the polarity, are hereditary in the sense that no-one not born of, for example, washerman parents, may practise the trade of washerman.

The general and permanent level for the caste is one thing, the individual's condition is another. That can vary consideraably at different times without his caste membership being affected, and normally does for a Brahmin in the course of the average day. As the representative of the purest human condition he is more exposed to the dangers of temporary impurity than others. Physical contact with, or even close proximity to, an untouchable defiles him.[1] He becomes what he eats and almost all organic substances are in varying degrees impure for him, consequently eating is a time of danger and even if his food has been prepared according to ritual and no accidents occur usually

'he rises from the table less pure than when he sat down'.[2]

Food and its exchange are associated in various ways with caste status (see pages 178-9). There are common pollution situations which affect everyone at some time. Menstruation pollutes women, and births and deaths pollute close relatives, who must for specified periods withdraw, like untouchables, from society.

Temporary pollution of the quotidian sort is dealt with by purificatory ritual which the individual himself can manage, particularly by lustration with water. Other agents of purification include various products of the cow, particularly butter and urine. The more serious temporary pollutions can only be cleansed with the aid of various ritual specialists. These specialists will also be called in when an individual or group wishes to rise to a level of purity requisite for a particular situation, usually a ceremony of some kind, such as a wedding.

Two other concepts which give meaning to and support the system are signalled by the words dharma and kharma. The first refers to established order, both cosmic and social, and more specifically to the code of ethics and duty peculiar to each caste. A man must live by his appropriate code in order to acquire merit. Merit is expounded in the doctrine of kharma, ethical metempsychosis. If a man acquires merit he is reborn in a higher stratum, if he violates his dharma he is reborn lower down. By correct observances in his successive reincarnations he may finally obtain release from the wheel of deaths and rebirths. It follows that as Srinivas aptly puts it, a man's caste position is an index of the state of his soul.[3] Max Weber in particular stressed

[1] Hutton, op. cit., p. 69. [2] Dumont, op. cit., p. 77.
[3] Srinivas, op. cit.

the significance of these ideas both as sanctions maintaining the system and as prompting the Indian spirit in an other-worldly direction.[1] Some modern students however feel that he over emphasized their significance.[2]

Consider again the description of Indian society as composed of four varna, including in it the purity-impurity polarity. It is clear that it does not present an accurate picture of the caste system and some authors have concluded that it is so far removed from an accurate picture that the best action is to ignore it. Most however have stressed its relevance to study of the caste system. Hocart,[3] Dumezil[4] and Dumont argue that the series of oppositions out of which it is constructed compose a pattern of norms basic to an understanding of relations among castes. As against the others the Brahmins are pure; as against the others Brahmins and kings wield power yet power is subordinate or complementary to purity; as against the others, the top three are twice born; and the whole comprises a unity against nature and the gods. Other features of the system can be adduced showing to what a remarkable extent it has

'the quality of a plan . . . endowed with meaning and purpose'.[5]

The number four (the number of the varna) is more than a mere number, it is an organizing principle in many spheres of knowledge and, ideally at any rate, for the life cycle of the individual. Hindu psychology or ethics postulates four main intentions or movements of the spirit, ranked in order of worth and associated with the appropriate varna:[6] towards release or salvation, towards sacrifice and righteousness, towards pleasure, and towards wealth. In cosmology four eons are recognized, starting with a Golden Age and mutating into a Lead Age of discord, which we now inhabit. There are four stages in the life cycle (after puberty) of a man: that of the celibate student devoted to study and right conduct; next of the householder immersed in worldly cares; then of the middle aged man beginning to retire and resuming his earlier studies and meditations; lastly of the Sannyasi, the holy beggar who renounces society, home and kin, and bends his spirit towards God.[7]

[1] M. Weber, *The Religion of India*. Free Press (1958).

[2] See, for example, L. Dumont, 'World Renunciation in Indian Religion', *Contributions to Indian Sociology*, no. 4, 1960. Also, K. Gough, 'Caste in a Tenjore Village', *Aspects of Caste*, ed. E. R. Leach. Cambridge (1960).

[3] A. M. Hocart, *Caste: A Comparative Study*. London (1950).

[4] G. Dumezil, *Mitra-Varuna*. Paris (1940).

[5] P. 10 above.

[6] I find different authorities sometimes differ on this point, some attaching release to the Brahmin, some to the Sannyasi.

[7] 'God' is probably wrong here; I merely give the Christian equivalent.

The varna represents a model of Indian society intended to be applicable everywhere throughout India. As such it has somewhat the same kind of validity as Marx's model of capitalist society, or the three class system we sometimes use to describe British society, of upper, middle and working class. It sketches in the background of norms, standards and meanings by reference to which Indians can orient themselves in diverse situations, and it provides standards by reference to which castes can claim positions in local rank orders.

Caste and occupation

The caste system is not an image of the economic division of labour. In the first place not all occupations are either pure or impure. Farming for example is neutral, though highly regarded, while many occupations such as oil pressing, though also neutral, are regarded as merely undignified, but not as polluting. These neutral occupations are ranked in terms of prestige much as occupations in our society are. Trading by and large is neutral as an activity, but it has the drawback of forcing a man into undesirable contacts. Epstein reports that in a village she studied the Peasant caste, the dominant landowners, regarded a shop as a goldmine but refused to take to trade as

'it would never do for a Peasant to squat on the floor of his shop and offer goods to passers by, who might be of lower caste or even untouchables. A Muslim can do this but not a Peasant!'[1]

As the illustration indicates, a fair amount of trading is done by non-Hindu sects, including Christians, who nevertheless in any local community are placed by the Hindus somewhere in the local caste hierarchy.

Some of the crafts are also neutral and the castes practising them, though placed within the general one, are ranked in terms of another hierarchy, an auspicious-inauspicious polarity. For example, iron is black hence inauspicious, so Blacksmiths rank below Silversmiths, who in turn are below Goldsmiths. D. Pocock notes that the rank of these castes is also correlated with the extent of the network of exchanges they are involved in. A blacksmith is involved in a restricted village network, a goldsmith in an extended or urban one.[2]

An individual's caste membership is not in any way affected by the amount of money he makes in his craft or occupation. Instances are reported of individual Untouchables becoming quite rich by, for

[1] S. T. Epstein, *Economic Development and Social Change in South India.* Manchester (1962), p. 33.

[2] See D. Pocock, 'Sociologies Urban and Rural', *Contributions to Indian Sociology,* no. 4, 1960. Also 'Notes on Jajmani Relationship', *Contributions to Indian Sociology,* no. 6, 1962.

example, running a bus service, but they remain Untouchables.[1] More important, a caste's status is not necessarily altered by an increase in the wealth of its members, though a jati may use or try to use wealth to raise its status (see page 80).

It is perhaps as well in thinking about the matter to distinguish between occupation and useful work. A caste occupation, because it is part of a social division of labour, brings caste members into relations with members of other castes. Useful work which one does for oneself does not, hence one can do a certain amount of useful work which comprises the occupations of other castes. For example, Mayer reports that in Malawi housewives regularly wash the household's clothes; they do not lose status by it but they would if they washed clothes for other households, especially in other castes.[2] Similarly to catch fish for oneself is undignified (probably prohibited for Brahmins), while to catch fish to exchange or sell is a low caste occupation.

Again, though many occupations are a hereditary right and duty of particular castes, some are not. This is particularly so of farming and some crafts. Members of all castes own land which they may farm themselves or rent to others, and members of all but the Brahmin caste may earn a living as farm labourers. Among the crafts mentioned above, including carpentry, members can if market conditions favour it switch from one to another. Practices such as this are probably not just a modern trend promoted by the expansion of a market economy. Pocock remarks that the traditional Hindu term for a guild, sereni, means

'a group of people of different castes that subsist by the occupation of one caste'.[3]

Finally, sometimes subcastes within a caste practise different occupations, even though the caste may bear a common occupational name. Segments of a caste within a locality may also give themselves slightly different names though practising the same occupation, e.g. Left Hand Potters and Right Hand Potters. However, as Dumont points out this subject requires more investigation than it has so far received, for sometimes the different occupations are merely superficial variations in procedure in the same occupation;[4] in other words subcastes or jati sometimes use these superficial differences to mark a separation arrived at on quite other grounds, simply because occupational specialization is the language in which caste differentiation is coded.[5] This may be further elucidated in the following section.

[1] See S. Dube, *Indian Village*. Routledge, London (1955).
[2] Mayer, op. cit., p. 53.
[3] Pocock, 'Sociologies Urban and Rural', op. cit.
[4] Dumont, op. cit., pp. 123–8.
[5] C. Lévi-Strauss, *La Pensée Sauvage*. Plon, Paris (1964), chap. 4.

Jati and segmentation

By endogamy is meant a ban on marriage outside a given group, so that group membership depends on descent from two parents already members of it. There is general agreement among scholars that the caste is not the endogamous unit in the system, but that the latter is the much smaller local section of the caste, the subcaste or the jati.[1]

'Every jati, or members of a jati in a particular village or group of neighbouring villages, constitutes a caste court which punishes caste offences'.[2]

Caste offences include engaging in wrong, i.e. lower status occupations, eating the wrong foods, or eating with forbidden castes, but perhaps the most serious is contracting a wrong marriage, for which the punishment may be excommunication, expulsion from the jati. Jati within a caste are themselves ranked, at least to some extent, or may dispute relative rank. Finally a jati is itself further segmented, although into groups of a different order, viz. exogamous lineages.

The segmentary nature of the system has often been commented on, whereby

'Lage divisions are subdivided into smaller ones, which are subdivided into smaller ones.'[3]

A. Bétaille found among ninety-two Brahmin households in one village no fewer than twelve named endogamous groupings, each referred to as a jati (with Brahmins as a whole also referred to as a jati). The divisions were connected mainly with doctrinal, ritual and functional differences. Throughout India temple priests are distinguished from those who serve other castes in household ritual. The subdivisions within a caste have closer and more distant ties with each other, so that in caste A, subdivisions A^1 and A^2 will consider themselves in some contexts as one unit superior to A^3 and A^4 as regards commensality, for example, while the whole caste will consider itself a unit superior to caste B, as regards commensality and in the context of village politics. To outsiders all members of a caste have equal status, while within it segments rank each other to greater or lesser degree. The 'fissiparous tendencies'[4] in the system result to some extent partly from the intrusion, in a peasant society in which interaction among individuals is largely confined to narrow localities, of the territorial factor into social organization, and partly from a tendency inherent in probably any status hierarchy for units in the system to compete for higher relative status. But more important, fission is closely connected with marriage, concubinage, and both upward and downward social

[1] Mayer, op. cit., should be consulted on this topic.
[2] Srinivas, op. cit., p. 24.
[3] A. Bétaille, *Caste Class and Power*. University of California Press (1965), p. 73.   [4] Hutton, op. cit., pp. 51–2.

mobility. In peasant societies marriage has consequences for the redistribution of property through inheritance and endowment in one or other of its forms.[1] In India a primary bride normally has to have a dowry. The marriage ceremony is a major one in the individual's life cycle.[2] A large assembly of guests have to be feasted, and for the bride's father it is the occasion of the heaviest expenditure in his life. It is probably the main source of peasant indebtedness.[3]

Now it is implicit in any hierarchical organization that equality of status means close association of some kind between those of equal status (or the possibility of it) and the exclusion from close association of those of lower status.[4] Correlatively, to enter into close association with those of lower status, with qualifications as to degree and frequency, is to lose status. It seems that universally marriage and commensality are the prime examples of close association which have implications for status.[5] Hindu marriage is moreover arranged by the two lineages of the couple and establishes enduring links between the families.[6] Both as to its expense and consequences for social relations, marriage is the occasion *par excellence* for the demonstration and preservation of status.

Apart from Brahmins, Indians do not by statute practise monogamy. However, they draw a distinction between primary marriage and secondary.[7] Primary marriage is the one that produces heirs, or full heirs, and confirms the status of the two lineages concerned; it is accordingly between status equals. The choice in secondary marriage is wider and need not be between equals. Further, there is no objection to a man having lower caste concubines.[8] Wives and children are

[1] For European peasants see, for example, the classic study by C. M. Arensberg, *The Irish Countryman*. London (1937).
[2] Srinivas, op. cit.
[3] See, for example, E. R. Leach, *Pul Eliya*. Cambridge (1961).
[4] See pp. 109, 120 for examples in modern society. For examples of the principle in industrial organizations see T. Burns and G. Stalker, *The Management of Innovation*. London (1961).
[5] As Weber remarked, *Essays in Sociology*, trs. Gerth and Mills. Routledge, London (1948), pp. 187–8.
[6] There are variations over India regarding this. A useful introduction to the subject is I. Karve, *Kinship Organization in India*. Poona (1953).
[7] Dumont, op. cit. (   ), pp. 144–63. The author notes that there is not full agreement among specialists on this and related points.
[8] G. D. Berremen speaks of low-caste women being sexually exploited; see his 'Comparative Analysis of Caste', p. 66, in *Caste and Race*, eds. A. Reuck and J. Knight. Churchill, London (1967). This situation seems to be normal in strongly stratified societies. For an example from preliterate societies see J. J. Maquet, *The Premise of Inequality in Ruanda*. UP (1961). Many publications treat of the subject in Victorian England. If we no longer enjoy or suffer the situation in contemporary Britain, our solutions, for example, the blurring of the distinction between wives and other women, are not without their attendant problems.

ranked accordingly, and the disinherited (in the case of concubines' children) or less privileged (in the case of secondary wives) may form a lower status subcaste. Thus, Mayer reports of the Farmer caste of Ramkheri that it contains an outcaste subcaste composed, it is said, of children of Rajput caste men and their Farmer servant girls.[1]

This is fission by downward mobility. Subcastes may also form through the upward mobility of a local segment either within the caste or beyond it (see page 80). Several intermarrying lineages of a sub-caste may decide to raise their status by refusing marriage and com-mensality to subcaste fellows and by altering their customs. If they are really serious they offer their daughters, as brides with splendid dowries, to a higher subcaste, even to one in a different caste. When it receives brides back from the latter it is then equal in status to it. Hypergamous relations between two units may thus be temporarily, or more permanently, associated with secondary marriage. Of course, not all jati are in a position to acquire the wealth needed to provide dowries expensive enough for upward mobility. The most important point here is that as a result of attempts at upward mobility the boundaries between two castes may, at a particular time and in a particular place, be difficult to discern.

Caste and community

Much of the complex of relationships making up the caste system is best studied in the context of the village or group of villages. These relationships are usually described, as recommended by Bouglé, in terms of the three categories of separation, hierarchy and interdependence.[2] Most of the preceding account comes under the heading of the first two. In addition, the physical layout of the village and residential patterns within it to some extent reflect social structure. Members of a jati tend to be neighbours and often streets are named after them. However, there is rarely an exact correspondence between the two and villages vary greatly in this respect.[3] Always, however, two groups stand out as clearly demarcated from the others, the Brahmins and the Untouchables, the latter normally inhabiting a separate hamlet some distance from the village proper. They are forbidden to use the wells others drink from and are barred from temples and other public buildings. Diet is to some extent correlated with caste, almost all Brahmin jati being vegetarian. Below them some castes eat mutton but not pork, and below pork eaters come beef eaters. Use of alcohol increases the lower the group. These differences are also bound up with the aspect of hierarchy. Differences in dress, diet

[1] Mayer, op. cit., pp. 154-6.
[2] C. Bouglé, *Essais sur le Régime des Castes*. Paris (1927).
[3] Compare the maps in Mayer, op. cit., pp. 54-5 with that in A. Bétaille, op. cit., p. 27.

and speech are, as in our society, indices of social position, and along
with discontinuities in relationships result in a

'tendency of each jati to live in a separate social world'.[1]

As an introduction to the aspect of hierarchy we may note the phenomenon of reversal of it.

Local hierarchy

The lowest group in the whole system is that of the Unseeables,
numerically sparse and found in only a few places. They are thought
to wash the clothes of other Untouchables. The latter at least enter
the village while social life is going on, but Unseeables may not and
should drag a branch behind them to obliterate footsteps. M. Banks
remarks:

'To an appreciable extent (Unseeables) still only flit about at twilight
and many (of other castes) are not even aware of their existence.'[2]

However, they have a formidable reputation as sorcerers who will kill
for a fee. The lowest, most impure group has the strongest evil power.
Reversals of position in popular thought are common in hierarchical
social systems, the poor having more chance of entry into heaven than
the rich. Poverty and labour are honest while money is the root of all
evil and power corrupts. The inverse symmetry of the reversal in caste
society is perhaps rather neater. Thus Bétaille remarks that if Untouchables are unwelcome in the Brahmin quarter the opposite is also the
case, for they fear a Brahmin's presence in their street will result in
sterility among them. The lowest group by voluntary act imposes
death on the living, for a fee; the highest group involuntarily deprives
the unborn of life, without payment.

Reversal is also exhibited in some village festivals. Marriott gives a
graphic account of a festival of love celebrated in Uttar Pradesh in
which castes and sexes co-operate in dramatic reversals of normal roles.
Women beat men; low caste beats high caste; a Water Carrier, a Barber's
son and two young Brahmins, normally 'avid experts in the daily
routines of purification',[3] spend the day hilariously throwing mud at
all the leading citizens. For a day cosmic order is destroyed, the moral
order polluted, to be re-created and repurified for another year.

A local hierarchy becomes visible through interaction among members
of different jati, particularly through rules regulating commensality

---

[1] Srinivas, op. cit., p. 24. Note however the reversals and interdependence
described in the following paragraphs.
[2] M. Banks, 'Caste in Jaffna', ed. in Leach, *Aspects of Caste in South India,
Ceylon and North West Pakistan*, Cambridge (1962), p. 65.
[3] McKinn Marriott, 'The Feast of Love', in *Krishan, Myths, Rites and
Attitudes*, ed. M. Singer, Honolulu (1966).

among jati. These are complex, applying in different ways to different categories of food (e.g. cooked and raw), to water, to smoking, and to various kinds of utensils in which food and water can be offered, metal or earthenware for example. Mayer has reduced the rules to a general formula:

> 'The position of a caste in the commensal hierarchy can be assessed on the principle that eating the food cooked or served by another caste denotes equality with it, or inferiority; and that not to eat denotes equality or superiority. Those castes which are most exclusive eat from nobody else, and the lowest castes eat from nearly everyone.'[1]

This leaves room for a certain amount of ambiguity; two jati may not eat with each other, the implication being that they are equal, while a third may accept food from one and not the other, implying that the first is the higher. Jati dispute their relative rankings to some extent, especially in the middle reaches of the system. This in no way destroys the caste hierarchy for as Bouglé pointed out disputes for precedence in their origin presuppose hierarchy and in their progress strengthen it.[2]

There are two important points about these local hierarchies: (a) invariably Brahmins are at the top and Untouchables at the bottom. A few other castes, particularly Barbers and Washermen, occupy relatively fixed positions such that the varna model is usually discernible in local hierarchies;[3] (b) in every village or locality there is a dominant caste, one which owns most of the land, is often numerically larger than any of the others, is wealthier than any other, and politically more powerful. Yet the dominant caste is not unusually Brahmin, though in some villages Brahmins, as well as being the highest status group, are also the dominant caste.[4] Here is an illustration of the normal situation, the hierarchy in Wangala, a village in Mysore (p. 80).

The dominant caste occupies the position of king in the varna model, and like a king it in a general way runs the village. The dominant caste is not a particular caste. The name is one given by anthropologists to whichever caste unit in a locality occupies that position. It follows from much that has been described so far that apart from Brahmins and untouchables castes do not occupy the same positions, relative to each other, in every local hierarchy. To some extent this is due to variations in local economies or in population density—not every one of Hutton's three thousand castes is represented in each village. It is also due to the fact that in the middle reaches of the system where

---

[1] Mayer, op. cit., pp. 33–4.
[2] Bouglé, op. cit.
[3] See, for example, G. D. Berreman, 'The Study of Caste Ranking in India', *S.W.J.A.*, no. 21, 1965. Observe particularly the footnote on p. 126.
[4] An example of such a village is described by Gough, op. cit.

there are a fair number of neutral occupations and jati may dispute position, status can be claimed and validated on several grounds: diet, occupation, marriage patterns and commensal exchanges all count. Finally, upward mobility by local jati also produces variations.

Bailey describes how one local jati acquired the wealth to move up. The Distiller caste in Bissipara about the middle of the nineteenth

TABLE TWO

Wangala population and landholding by caste*

Hierarchy	Households		Landholding (Wangala and elsewhere	
	Number	per cent	Acres	per cent
Lingayat priest (Saivite)	3	1·70	9·00	1·40
Peasant	128	66·50	562·00	88·90
Potter	4	2·10	5·50	1·20
Goldsmith	5	2·70	4·00	0·50
Blacksmith	4	2·10	3·75	0·50
Fisherman	4	2·10	1·00	0·20
Madras peasant (1)	3	1·70	—	—
Madras peasant (2)	2	1·00	—	—
Washerman	2	1·00	1·50	0·20
Muslim	2	1·00	2·00	0·40
Untouchable (A.K.)	28	14·60	42·75	6·70
Untouchable (Vodda)	7	3·50	—	—
Total	192	100·00	631·50	100·00

* From Epstein, op. cit., p. 24. Other examples can be found in works cited above.

century occupied a relatively low position just above the Untouchables. The dominant caste was that of the Warrior. Increase in their numbers, along with inheritance rules stipulating that all sons inherit, led to fragmentation of their estates to the point where many holdings became unprofitable and the owner was forced to sell. Meanwhile the Distillers, taking advantage of new government liquor laws and the enlarged market opened up by the *pax Brittanica* and more extended communication, were able to accumulate money which they invested in buying warriors' land, a source both of income and prestige. Through their caste council new rules of behaviour were promulgated, e.g. members were forbidden to eat meat or drink alcohol, in imitation of Brahmins. Backsliders were punished, for persuading other castes to accept their claim to higher status required a disciplined campaign. The Distillers now challenge the Warriers for the position of dominant caste and attempt to dominate the village council, the instrument of local government.[1]

[1] Bailey, op. cit.

It seems that in the past the position of dominant caste could be won by sheer force, violence or the threat of it, as kingdoms once were. Village dominant castes are in fact sometimes linked in various ways to the royal linage which until recently reigned over the kingdom the village belonged to. This raises the question as to the place of force or violence in the caste system. Though relations between castes are defined in custom, and alterations in details of relations can be negotiated in discussion between caste councils, violence is never far below the surface in the regulation of intercaste affairs, at least as between the dominant caste and lower ones. Cohn for example describes how when members of an Untouchable caste in one village managed to improve their economic and political position somewhat members of the dominant caste attacked them physically and confiscated some of their property.[1] Lower castes, and especially jati bent on moving up, sometimes attempt to display symbols of higher status. The extent to which violence is used to prevent them is not known, but a recent report records a case of three Untouchables being shot dead for curling their moustaches upwards.[2]

Finally, before turning to interdependence, jati mobility is not something exceptional but a normal feature of the caste system.[3] At some time or place every caste will be found to have a local segment in the position of dominant caste. To claim or demand higher status is one thing, to have the claim accepted by others is another; how the position is validated is described below. It seems though that formerly it was one of the duties of the king to ratify the position of a new dominant caste, which he did by solemnly announcing that of course it was not really a new position, the dominant caste had merely reassumed its ancient and rightful position. Hence our received picture of unchanging India. The received picture is of course correct in so far as this kind of change in no way alters the social structure.[4]

Interdependence

Colourful village ceremony, as in the festival of love referred to previously, is one context in which integration through interdependence

---

[1] B. S. Cohn, 'The Changing Status of a Depressed Caste', *Village India*, ed. McKinn Marriott. *A.A.*, vol. 57, no. 3, part 2, memoir no. 83, June 1955. See also K. Gough, op. cit., who emphasizes the repressive aspects of the system.

[2] *The Times*, Tues., 16 January 1968.

[3] G. M. Carstairs, *The Twice Born*. London (1957). He speaks of a continual upward movement on the part of the lower castes, causing irritation and feelings of insecurity among the higher.

[4] D. Pocock, 'The Movement of Castes', *Man*, no. 79, 1955. Also, D. Pocock, 'The Antropology of Time Reckoning', *Contributions to Indian Sociology*, no. 7, 1964. R. Lingat, 'Time and the Dharma', *Contributions to Indian Sociology*, no. 6, 1962. L. Dumont, 'Kingship in Ancient India', *Contributions to Indian Sociology*, no. 6, 1962.

F

becomes apparent. This kind of dramatic mobilization of castes is, however, less important than the continuous organization of relationships among caste members in the community known as the jajmani system.[1]

It is a system of service exchanges and redistribution linking higher and lower caste families in patron-client relations (usually called jajman-kamin), and linking some lower caste families in either further patron-client relations or in gift exchanges. Links between families are hereditary in most cases but can be broken off by mutual consent. One must remember that the dominant caste is, if not invariably numerically preponderant, usually fairly large. Families of lower castes such as Carpenters, Blacksmiths, Potters, Water Carriers, Washermen, Basket makers, Cooks, Sweepers, etc., provide services and products to patron families among the higher castes, mainly of the dominant caste and of the Brahmins. In addition Brahmins provide services to dominant caste families and perhaps to a few other castes of relatively high status. Many of the Untouchables, whatever their traditional caste occupation, provide labour at the appropriate seasons on higher caste farms. Formerly (before 1843) many were in the position of serfs, i.e. subject to punishment if they tried to run away, or to change masters without the permission of their patron.[2]

In return patrons have to give customarily fixed recompense, mostly in produce and concessions of various kinds, to their clients. These latter include areas of rent free land, free house land, trees, etc. Recompense takes many forms as regards frequency, value and type of product: grain, butter, milk, clothing, etc., are given yearly, seasonally, monthly or daily. At present money is sometimes also used in recompense.

In addition to the regular services they have agreed to, clients are bound to serve their patrons in household ritual at births, marriages and deaths,[3] Their duties on these occasions are complex in detail and variable over India as a whole. Examples are: Genealogists who are also astrologers chart auspicious moments and draw up horoscopes; Washermen purify clothes and Barbers mens' bodies, and barbers' wives the womens' bodies; and Untouchables such as Drummers and Dancers provide entertainment, or carry torches at funerals. The lower castes' functions are in general to absorb pollution from the higher,

---

[1] There are many accounts, or partial accounts, of this system in the literature cited above. In addition, the classic account is by W. H. Wiser, *The Hindu Jajmani System*. N.Y. (1959). A useful review of recent work is in P. M. Kolenda, 'Towards a Model of the Hindu Jajmani System', *Human Organization*, vol. 1, 1963. Reprinted in *Tribal and Peasant Economics*, ed. Dalton. N.Y. (1967). Both these reviews were written before the publication of Epstein, op. cit., which is essential to an understanding of the system.

[2] K. Gough, op. cit.

[3] Srinivas, op. cit., gives detailed descriptions and analyses of these.

so maintaining the relative purity of the latter. Many of these lower castes are, if not exactly priests, then essential functionaries in a liturgy which in varying degree or frequency encompasses all castes in mutual religious interdependence.

Though we distinguish one kind of service as economic and the other as religious Indians describe them all in the same terms as rights and obligations of jajman and kamin. As in all patron-client relations the two are expected to support each other in public life, the patron arguing his client's cases in disputes brought to the village council, the client offering his strong right arm in support of his patron should factional quarrels within the dominant caste erupt in violence. Regulation of patron-client relations is another area of operation of subcaste councils.

There is some discussion amongst scholars as to whether or not the system is universal throughout India, on the scope of contractual economic relations in it as against hereditary ties and fixed customary rewards, and correlatively, on the place of money in exchange. Disagreements are to some extent due to: (a) some scholars emphasizing the economic content of patron-client ties to the exclusion of the religious; (b) to regional or district variations in agriculture. For example, where the dominant caste grow a cash crop, recompense may be largely in money without the amount of payment being affected by market relations of supply and demand; (c) to differences among castes in the extent to which a caste occupation lends itself to market or jajmani relationships, e.g. a Barber or a Potter may not serve lower castes, especially Untouchables, as he would become impure to their level if he did so. The neutral trades mentioned above, however, can enter into exchange with all other castes. Their 'natural' context is the market.

The system has been differently interpreted by different scholars. Hocart treated it as a religious division of labour although he assumed as a matter of common sense that religious services have to be paid for.[1] It is to Hocart that we owe the first formulation of the principle explaining the dominant caste's position, and accordingly also how a new one validates its position. The dominant caste, Hocart said, is the caste which can afford to pay for all the services available in the system. Wiser and Beidelman give more attention to the economic aspects of the relationships, but whereas the former stresses mutuality of relations and the harmony of the whole, the latter stresses inequalities of political and economic power and speaks of it as a system of exploitation and coercion.

Study of the matter has been placed on a new level by the work of S. T. Epstein, who shows that the three interpretations are not

---

[1] Hocart, op. cit.

irreconcilable, each stressing a particular facet of the system.[1] Having
collected quantitative data on output and distribution of crops in two
villages, she analyses the landowner-labourer relation as follows. As
in all peasant economies crop output fluctuates from one year to another
according to weather. A good harvest is four times the quantity of a
bad. In a bad year the total output of the village is slightly more than
enough to keep all households fed, provided it is distributed equally
among all of them. Yet there is great discrepancy in landholding between
the Peasant dominant caste and its clients the Untouchables. The
average Peasant holding is four acres, the average Untouchable holding
one and a half acres. The average Peasant house needs a minimum of
one hundred and twenty labour days to cultivate its land, requiring
two labourers at least. As measurements of individual effort and
productivity are impossible, the Peasant famer takes as the standard
of payment the average product per labourer in a bad year. This
average product is found by simply sharing the output equally among
all the cultivators.

> 'In bad years Wangala villagers, Peasants and their dependent
> households alike, all received an equal share of the total quantity
> of (grain) produced.'[2]

In bad years the masters received no more than the untouchables.

In the years of bumper crops, on the other hand, the dependent
labourers still receive the standard payment while the surplus belongs
to the master. This he uses to finance feasts, weddings and rituals
from which he wins prestige, or to buy new bullocks or repair his
house. In other words there is equal distribution in bad years and
unequal in good. Untouchables accept the system because of the
security it affords them in bad years, and masters because it ensures
them a supply of labour in good years when, because of the extent
and weight of the crop, labour is badly needed. The master's conspicuous consumption also benefits the lower castes, as they receive a
share at feasts and payments for their parts in ritual. The annual
rewards for craftsmen are also fixed regardless of the amount of service.
The three facets of the system separately emphasized by the three
authors mentioned fall into place in a unitary system in this analysis.
Epstein's work also illustrates well the operation of a natural or non-
market economy, in which personal relations of dependency between
men of different status groups takes the place of contract relations of
the market.

[1] Epstein, op. cit. Also S. T. Epstein, 'Productive Efficiency and Customary
Systems of Rewards in Rural South India', *Themes in Economic Anthropology*,
ed. R. Firth. London (1967), pp. 229–52.
[2] Epstein, 'Productive Efficiency and Customary Systems of Rewards in
Rural South India', op. cit., pp. 242–3.

Theories of caste

One theory of caste, popular at the beginning of the century but still current in some quarters, links it with ethnic differences and race relations. A statement of it by Hutton may be summarized thus. Originally India was populated by endogamous tribes managing relations among themselves in terms of food taboos and other mystical notions. Light skinned Aryan invaders, their social organization already characterized by stratification, enforced their rule on the aboriginals. The fusion of stratification, conquest and primitive exclusivism resulted in the caste system.[1] Max Weber lent the authority of his prestige to some ideas in the ambience of a racial theory by linking caste with ethnic segregation. He rejected a conception of the caste system as simply an economic division of labour exhibiting a high degree of stratification by class (market position), and treated castes as status groups ranked according to the degree of social honour accorded them. His concept of social honour, however, was somewhat ambiguous. On the one hand it was a synonym for prestige, a regard or estimation accorded a group by the community at large, and on the other hand it was a synonym for a unique style of life and culture, something members of a culturally distinct group shared with each other irrespective of what other groups in the community thought about it. Turning to Europe for comparable phenomena Weber pointed out that ethnically distinct groups within a European nation unusually have in some degree a distinctive culture and are liable to be endogamous in fact if not in law; his example was the Jews in Germany. It was, Weber held, the combination of ethnic segregation and status group ranking which resulted in caste.

Weber's proposed analogy is not very exact. A caste is not found isolated, an island in the ocean of an alien culture. He somewhat exaggerated religious differences among castes, remarking that each had its separate god, a view emphatically rejected by modern students. Ritual interdependence is an outstanding feature of the system. Moreover, there are between two thousand and three thousand castes and surely not that number of ethnically distinct groups in India. What, in any case, would the theory explain? At the most it would account for the aspect of separation between castes, but not for the aspect of interdependence and systematic hierarchical integration. As Cox remarks:

> 'All attempts to rank castes in India according to physical criteria have proved fruitless, and . . . none of the researchers has been able to state his hypothesis clearly, nor has he been able to show the significance of the same for an understanding of the caste system.'[2]

---

[1] Hutton, op. cit.
[2] O. Cox, *Caste, Class and Race.* N.Y. (1948), p. 108.

Cox's criticisms, however, are directed mainly against a more modern variant of the theory expounded by some American sociologists, who interpret the Indian caste system and relations between negroes and whites in America within the same frame of reference.[1] The word varna means colour, and each varna is associated with one, Brahmins with white, for example, and Sudras with black. The two ethnic groups in America are declared to be castes, separated by endogamy, ranking as superior and inferior, and on the part of the superior by feelings, if not concepts, regarding contacts which resemble the tone of the idea of pollution. There are however many differences between the two situations. The Hindu colours do not refer to skin pigmentation but symbolize functions in the varna model. Warriors are appropriately associated with red but no one expects them to have red skins. On the other hand, neither whites nor negroes are as groups occupationally specialized, even though the proportion of poor (unskilled labourers) among negroes is higher than among whites. Economic exchange between them is not organized through patron-client relations nor bound up with religious duties, and mobility within each is accomplished by individuals or families, not by ascriptive groups such as jati. Finally, theories of racial superiority and Hindu religion could be said to be the same only on the grounds that both are equally mistaken, a super-ficial equation and a crass simplification of the concept of ideology. Discrimination against negroes contradicts the doctrines of natural right incorporated in the American constitution, whereas Indian society is based on an institutionalization of inequality.[2]

There are, however, two points to note in connection with ethnic segregation or racial theories. First, there are tribal or tribal-like popula-tions in India who retain in greater or lesser degree some kind of independence from the caste system. They inhabit the more isolated less fertile areas, and are usually somewhat unsophisticated as regards religion and economic organization. One general process in Indian history has been the incorporation of these populations into caste society.[3] Some castes bear a tribal, not occupational, name. Second, at present there can often be observed striking differences in skin colour and appearance between many Brahmins, non-Brahmins and untouchables.[4] Whether these physical differences are to be attributed to race or to differences in diet and occupation is problematical, but these, along with uncritical acceptance of the race account of Indian history, do suffice to render credible in outline a racialist interpretation

[1] G. D. Berreman, 'Caste in India and the US', *American Journal of Sociology*. September 1960.
[2] L. Dumont, 'Caste, Racism and Stratification', *Contributions to Indian Sociology*, no. 5, 1961. See also correspondence between Dumont and Berreman in *Contributions to Indian Sociology*, no. 6, 1962, pp. 120–5.
[3] On this subject see F. Bailey, *Tribe, Caste and Nation*, Manchester (1960).
[4] Bétaille, op. cit., pp. 48–50.

for those who seek one. Some Brahmin groups now propound the theory as ideological support for elitist political programmes.

Economic interpretations of caste society take various forms, and perhaps all they have in common is a relegation of its religious significance to a position of secondary importance. One of the earliest was that the system is merely a variant of guild organization as found in medieval Europe. Weber amongst others, however, listed several decisive differences, e.g. guilds were only rarely hereditary groups, nor were they by law or custom endogamous. There were no complex barriers to commensality among them nor equally complex ritual interdependence. Moreover, as many scholars have pointed out, guilds in any case appear early in Indian history, and though not wholly separate from the caste system are distinct from it. It has often been noted that both in the past and at present Indian guilds have been closely associated with sectarian movements cohering around heterodox religions or doctrines, particularly Buddhism and Jainism. These,

'though they did not directly attack the caste system, were nevertheless opposed to it and can, to that extent, be described as non-caste movements'.[1]

More recently Leach has proposed a model in terms of which interpretation might proceed. He regards economic interdependence stemming from a division of labour 'of a quite special type' as fundamental to the caste system.[2] This special type results from a socio-demographic complex peculiar to Indian society.

'It is characteristic of class-organized societies that rights of ownership are the prerogative of minority groups which form privileged elites. The capacity of the upper class minority to exploit the services of the lower class majority is critically dependent upon the fact that the members of the underprivileged group must compete among themselves for the favour of the elite. It is the specific nature of a caste society that this position is reversed. Economic roles are allocated by right to closed minority groups of low social status; members of the high status dominant caste to whom the low status groups are bound, generally from a numerical majority, must compete among themselves for the services of individual members of the lower castes.'[3]

In modern India this once clear cut structure of relations between dominant and lower classes has become obscured through population increase among the latter and a growing obsolescence of traditional occupations, so that now, in contrast to the caste system we find in

---

[1] R. Thakar, *History of India*. Penguin, Harmondsworth (1966), p. 68.
[2] E. R. Leach, 'What Shall We Mean By Caste?', op. cit.
[3] Ibid.

India the two antagonistic economic classes of unemployed proletariat and landowning capitalists. The landlords' former duty to maintain their servants has been abolished

'by arbitrary acts of liberal legislation extending over the past one hundred and fifty years'.[1]

Serfdom was abolished in 1843, but the main result was that the now rightless labourer lost security and failed to gain freedom. Money became the medium of exchange and labourers, in need of money during periods of unemployment, had to turn to their ex-masters for loans, thus becoming tied to them through debt instead of the former reciprocal rights and obligations.

The nature of the relationship between landlords and lower castes is somewhat obscure in this model. One would expect that competition among landlords for the services of the lower would have resulted in lower castes being able to bargain for much better terms than in fact they obtained. We know that serfs in Europe were often able to improve their position during times of labour shortage, e.g. after the Black Death. Finally, as in all economic interpretations of caste, the model hardly accommodates the fact that Brahmins everywhere rank highest in the caste hierarchy but are by no means everywhere the dominant or richest caste. Leach of course is deliberately eschewing an interpretation in terms of Weber's concept of castes as status groups, but perhaps too much is lost in doing so. However, the model does point to two important problems, the extent to which British occupation strengthened the position of the landowning castes,[2] and the extent to which classes in the Marxist sense are in process of formation in modern India. That they are in process of formation few scholars doubt.[3] The only question is to what extent, and in what contexts caste and class are the operative membership groups for Indians. As the market economy increases in scope the local community ceases to be the sole context in which economic and political relationships are articulated into a system controlling the behaviour and rewards of constituent units, subcastes or individuals. The topic is complex and data scarce, but it may safely be said that there are no signs yet of the caste system disappearing, a fate Marx held to be inevitable with the development of industry in India.[4]

<hr>

[1] E. R. Leach, 'What Shall We Mean by Caste?', op. cit.
[2] See Barrington Moore, *Social Origins of Dictatorship and Democracy*. A. Lane, London (1967).
[3] See A. Bétaille, op. cit.
[4] K. Ishwaran, *Shivapur*. London (1968), p. 180. He writes: 'The solidarity of caste is not crumbling either under the impact of federal legislation aiming to abolish it or under the impact of those technological, political and other changes impinging upon Shivapur from the outside'.

Functional theory and caste society

Caste society seems at first sight a perfect subject for functional analysis. By starting this account with a sketch of Hindu models and values I may seem to have been following the approach of Parsons. However, it has become clear in the course of the account that the system involves local control of the means of production and application of sanctions by a dominant caste, not moreover as something which intrudes into a system otherwise perfectly integrated by common values, but as essential to the system in which secular power is subordinate to purity.

In current American sociology the caste system is treated merely as an analogue of race relations in the USA or as a foil to illustrate by contrast the characteristics of the American class system.[1] The terms of the contrast are the ascription of status in closed groups (caste) as against acquisition of status in open groups (class). Lenski formulates the difference as

'upward mobility by individuals is socially legitimate where classes are involved, but not in the case of castes'.[2]

The implication here is that because the caste is a closed group the individual is not permitted to move out of it. It would, however, be more accurate to say that it is because the individual is not permitted that castes are closed groups, i.e. that membership in a caste (subcaste) is a certificate of citizenship in caste society. A person has rights and obligations only as a member of a caste, not as an individual.[3]

This becomes clearer if we consider the Sannyasi (see page 72) the most revered category in Hindu society. These are holy men who have renounced all social ties and rights and live solely by begging, on the charity of others. Though enjoying the highest social honour they do not form a caste, they have become individuals. Anybody can become one of the Sannyasi but the position has its dangers. Any attempt on the part of one to resume his former rights is punished by derogation to the level of Untouchable. A more correct formulation of the difference between American society and Hindu as regards individual mobility is accordingly that they stand in an inverse and opposite relation to it. In India only the highest group accepts anybody; failure to live up to its standards leads to derogation to the lowest group. In America only the lowest group, the underworld, accepts anybody; success in living up to its standards leads to transfer to the highest group, the millionaires.[4] From this we may understand the

[1] See, for example, B. Barber, *Social Stratification*. N.Y. (1957).
[2] Lenski, *Power and Privilege*. McGraw-Hill (1966).
[3] L. Dumont, 'The Modern Conception of the Individual', *Contributions to Indian Sociology*, no. 8, 1965.
[4] D. Bell, 'Crime as an American Way of Life', *Antioch Review*, vol. 8, 1953.

potency of the underworld as a symbol in the American imagination, and perhaps also the violence often said to be characteristic of American life.

I expect that a functionalist might argue here that only a small proportion of Hindus become Sannyasi, the majority do not, therefore caste and class differ as stated in Lenski's formulation. It is, however, simply not true that upward mobility by individuals is illegitimate in caste society. On the contrary, the individual is specifically enjoined to acquire merit in order to be reborn higher up the system.[1] If the functionalist were now to argue that metempsychosis is impossible therefore, objectively speaking, there is no upward mobility apart from the Sannyasi, he could only do so by ignoring Hindu values, the desirability of merit, of becoming a Brahmin and eventually nothing, and also Hindu knowledge. To ignore the first is to run counter to functionalist methodology, to ignore the second is implicitly to turn current Western knowledge into an absolute standard by reference to which other systems of knowledge are merely incorrect, hence irrelevant, an ethnocentric attitude which neither furthers enlightenment nor aids understanding.

[1] One can probably ascertain from an astrologer who one has been, and hence how one is progressing with regard to mobility.

5

Modern Society

ACCORDING to Marx the main contradiction in capitalism which would initiate the process and events ending in its destruction was the discrepancy between its productive capacity and the capacity of society to absorb that production. Income is distributed in such a way that the mass of the population cannot purchase all that the system produces. This results in periodic and recurring crises of overproduction, each temporarily solved by a sudden decrease in production, which in turn results in unemployment among the proletariat and bankruptcy among the smaller, financially weaker firms. Marx thought that these crises would progressively increase in severity with ever increasing numbers of people reduced to pauperdom and ever fewer capitalists surviving to share the market among themselves or severally to monopolize particular sectors of it. Society, Marx anticipated, would become ever more clearly polarized into a small class of immensely rich monopoly capitalists and a huge mass of relatively impoverished proletariat; revolution would be almost inevitable.

Another destructive process he thought, if not perhaps a contradiction, was this. Profits are gained by the extraction of surplus value from labour; as machines replace men, and as in general the supply of new resources and markets diminishes, the rate of profit is bound to fall. Fields for profitable investment would shrink, with a consequent diminution of the power of capital. A further argument, developed by Rosa Luxemburg and Lenin among others, stated that competition among capitalist countries for decreasing markets would result in increasingly ferocious imperialist wars among them, and within each further promote the growth of monopolies. The former process would bring about conditions of chaos in which the forces of revolution would mature; the latter, cancelling the competition basic to the capitalist economic system, would prepare the way for the appropriation of enterprises by the state. These of course are simplified statements of intricately argued theses, but I have neither the space nor the competence to expound them more fully, nor to rehearse the theoretical counter arguments of non-Marxist economists.[1] What concerns sociologists is that Marx's predictions about the future of capitalist society

[1] See J. A. Schumpeter, *Capitalism, Socialism and Democracy*, N.Y. (1943).

have not been borne out in the major capitalist countries. In these there has not as yet been a proletarian revolution nor has society become polarized, at least not as he envisaged. True, there may yet be a revolution, but some explanation for its absence so far, an explanation as to why

'Capitalism has shown an unexpected vitality',[1]

is more relevant to our present understanding of stratification in our society than mere repetition of Marx's analysis followed by a hope or threat that in the long run events will prove it to have been correct. Since about the mid-thirties both Marxist and non-Marxist sociologists have debated why Marx's predictions regarding polarization and revolution have not been realized. All explanations start with a recognition of political, economic and social changes in capitalist countries since Marx wrote. Many commentators consider that as a result of these changes the term capitalist, in so far as it refers to the state of affairs Marx analysed, is now misleading as applied to the kind of society we now have, and a number of terms have been offered to replace it, e.g. the post-capitalist society, the affluent society, the industrial society, the consumer society, mass society, neocapitalist society. It is of course less important to pick and choose among them than to understand the changes they are meant to indicate.

(a) Changes in the division of labour

The early stages of industrialization are accompanied by the transfer of a large proportion of the working population from agriculture and related occupations to industrial production. Many small farmers and rural craftsmen become industrial labourers along with agricultural labourers. Later stages, however, are characterized by three inter-dependent processes. First, advances in science and technology both increase the scope of industrial production and render processes of production more complex, so that a more skilled labour force is required. Second, new science-based professions arise and some old occupations such as teaching expand in number and acquire the status of a profession.[2] Third, there is a transfer of a proportion of the working population from both agriculture and industry into the tertiary or service sector of the economy, the sector dominated by the white collar worker, clerks, bureaucrats, shop assistants, etc.[3] Consequences for the division of labour and the general form, to use a loose preliminary phrase, of the system of stratification are:

[1] M. Lefebvre, *The Sociology of Marx*. N.Y. 1968.
[2] See G. D. H. Cole, *Studies in Class Structure*. London (1955).
[3] See for example W. Rostow, *The Stages of Economic Growth*. Cambridge (1960).

(a) the number and variety of occupations increases; in 1851 the census of Great Britain identified 7,000 occupations, that of 1951 some 40,000;[1]

(b) the proportion of the population in skilled and semiskilled jobs increases at the expense of that in unskilled jobs;

(c) a new middle class of non-manual workers interposes itself between workers and capitalists.

Though the majority of the latter are proletariat in Marx's sense, owning no productive property, nevertheless they are distinguished from manual workers in style of life, attitudes and work situation. The magnitude of these general changes during this century alone in the USA and Britain are indicated in the following Table.

TABLE THREE

Percentage of occupied population in occupational groups, United States of America (1910–1950) and Great Britain (1911–1951)*

	USA GB	1910 1911	1920 1921	1930 1931	1940 —	1950 1951
Occupation	*Place*			*per cent*		
1 Professional and semi-professional	USA	4·4	5·0	6·1	6·5	7·5
	GB	4·1	4·3	4·4	—	6·1
2 Proprietors, managers, officials,	USA	23·0	22·3	19·9	17·8	16·3
	GB	10·4	10·7	10·6	—	10·6
of whom farmers	USA	16·5	15·5	12·4	10·1	7·5
	GB	1·6	1·8	1·6	—	0·0
Wholesale and retail dealers	USA	3·3	3·4	3·7	3·9	3·2
	GB	2·7	2·4	2·8	—	2·0
Others	USA	3·2	3·4	3·8	3·7	5·6
	GB	6·1	6·5	6·2	—	7·7
3 Clerical and kindred	USA	5·2	8·8	10·0	10·6	13·3
	GB	7·3	8·8	9·2	—	12·7
4 Sales	USA	5·0	5·0	6·3	6·6	6·9
	GB	5·7	4·7	6·1	—	5·4
5 Skilled workers and foremen	USA	11·7	13·5	12·9	11·7	13·8
	GB	13·9	15·7	15·0	—	16·8
6 Servant classes	USA	6·8	5·4	6·9	8·0	7·4
	GB	10·4	8·4	9·4	—	6·1
7 Farm labourers	USA	14·5	9·4	8·6	7·1	4·6
	GB	6·5	5·2	4·4	—	3·2
8 Semiskilled and unskilled workers not elsewhere classified	USA	29·4	30·7	29·3	31·7	30·2
	GB	41·7	42·2	40·9	—	39·1

* From G. Routh, *Occupation and Pay in Great Britain 1906–1960.* Cambridge (1965), p. 13.

Semiskilled and unskilled workers are not separated in this table.

[1] For further details see D. C. Marsh, *The Changing Social Structure of England and Wales.* London (1965), chap. 5.

K. Mayer gives the following estimate of changes in the distribution of population among the three manual grades in the USA 1910–1950: skilled workers as a proportion of the working population increase from 11·7 per cent to 13·8 per cent; semiskilled increase from 14·7 per cent to 19·8 per cent while unskilled decrease from 21·5 per cent to 16·5 per cent.[1]

The various grades of occupations compete with each other over the apportionment of the national income among them, i.e. each tries to raise its level of pay as against the others. Competition of this nature is of course quite different from class conflict in Marx's sense. Recent events in Poland would seem to indicate that occupational grades may still compete for income in some communist societies in which classes in Marx's sense have been abolished.[2] Moreover, the existence of several expanding layers of more highly paid non-manual occupations combined with the possibility of upward mobility offers the individual manual worker the possibility of escape from his position, or the hope that his children will achieve it, though the magnitude of the possibility and the extent to which the hope is realistic are of course subject to debate.

(b) Economic changes

Perhaps the most important has been economic growth, of which the processes mentioned above are concomitants. Real *per capita* income has increased throughout the working population, so that far from becoming impoverished in any absolute sense, the mass of the population enjoys a higher standard of living than did that of the mid-nineteenth century.[3] Marx was aware that poverty is relative and meant that the proletariat would become poorer relative to capitalists. However, if poverty is relative, we must know what standard of wealth people accept as a reference point from which to asses their own condition. Marxists have failed to deal with the problem, discussed below (see pages 136–140).

Crises in the trade cycle have at times interrupted but not stopped the process of economic growth. Moreover, through the application by governments of measures devised by economists the crises have to some extent been brought under control, so that for the last thirty years they have not had the devastating effects they formerly had.

A change much cited in critiques of Marx is that of the increasing separation of ownership and control in many large enterprises. Joint stock companies rather than private family businesses are now the rule, and shares in them are fairly widely distributed among the

[1] K. B. Mayer, *Class and Society*. N.Y. (1955), p. 76.
[2] See, for example, K. S. Karol, 'Workers' Power in Poland', *New Statesman*, 5 February 1971.
[3] See Aron, op. cit. Rostow, op. cit.

population. M. Postan remarks that in 11 major steel companies in 1963 capital was held by more than 275,000 shareholders; that the average shareholding was £885 a head in nominal value, and that more than 92 per cent of the shareholders held less than 1,000 shares each. Of the remaining 8 per cent the bulk was held not by private persons but by insurance companies, pension funds, unit trusts and trade unions.[1] The extent of this dispersal of capital is not known. Postan is careful to emphasize that it is doubtful whether it went far enough to affect by itself the distribution of wealth in the UK during the period he considers. Despite our ignorance much use has been made of the phenomenon by some recent proponents of the elite theory, who maintain that since ownership is dispersed among shareholders, control of the means of production has passed into the hands of managers whose interests diverge considerably from those of capitalists. Since capital is dispersed, they argue, we are no longer governed by a capitalist ruling class, but by an elite composed in whole or in part of the dominant managers in business and finance.

(c) Changes in the structure and functioning of the state

It is as well in considering these to recall that when Marx spoke of workers as being alienated from society, partly what he had in mind was that they were excluded from even the most exiguous participation in political activity:

'Even in Britain, often described as the classical instance of modern representative government, barely four per cent of the population took part in national elections before the reforms of 1885.'[2]

Since then suffrage has been extended to all adults, and political parties representing workers interests have been formed. Trade unions have been legally empowered to represent employees in bargaining with employers over wage rates, while the state has legislated extensively on such matters as working hours and safety and sanitary conditions in work places. The state can no longer be regarded simply as the institution whose main or sole function is to protect private property and to promote the interests of a particular class. This is partly because a political party, to achieve power, has to secure widespread support for its policies from the electorate, but also because the operations of the state have become intermeshed with the economic process and with institutions maintaining standards of education and health requisite for its efficient functioning. The state is itself a major owner of industrial

[1] M. M. Postan, *An Economic History of Western Europe, 1945-1964*. London (1967), p. 215.
[2] R. Dahrendorf, 'Recent Changes in the Class Structure of European Societies', *Daedalus*, Winter, 1964.

and service installations[1] and actively intervenes in the economic
process, controlling the trade cycle with varying degrees of success
and promoting policies of growth and low unemployment. As one
Marxist has stressed

'. . . a specific political autonomy is difficult to attribute to the state,
but a specifically economic autonomy is impossible to attribute to
the market. Indeed, the classical market has disappeared and has
been replaced not simply by structures of a monopolistic or oligo-
polistic sort but by a complicated apparatus of controlled, inter-
locking processes. The original (Marxian) notion of base and
superstructure has little meaning in the face of this concrete totality'.[2]

One of the most significant social processes involved in the extension
of the power and scope of operations of the state has been the extension
of rights of citizenship, lucidly analysed by T. H. Marshall.[3] By rights
of citizenship Marshall means those rights which accrue to a person
simply by virtue of being a citizen of the nation. They are of three
general sorts, civil, political and social. Civil rights are those necessary
for individual freedom: liberty of the person, freedom of speech
thought and faith, the right to own property and conclude contracts,
and the right to defend and assert these rights on terms of equality
with others by due process of law. Political rights are those which
empower a person to participate in the exercise of political power. In
Britain the major civil rights had become attached to the status of
citizen by the end of the eighteenth century, and the political rights
by the opening decades of the twentieth. Formal inequalities of status
have been abolished. During this century social rights have been added,
i.e. rights to a basic minimum of economic security, education and
health sufficient to enable a person to 'share in the social heritage'.
Partly as a result of these welfare provisions and partly as a result of
the fiscal measures instituted to provide finance for them, particularly
graduated income tax, many argue that distribution of real income is
either more equal than in the nineteenth century or such as to render
questionable any claim that relative poverty can be attributed unequi-
vocally to exploitation of a lower by a ruling class. Poverty, it has been
argued, is no longer class poverty but case poverty, a matter of individual casualties rather than a consequence of a particular socio-
economic structure.[4]

The arguments advanced as a critique of Marx and as accounting for
the proletariat's failure to fulfil the historic role he assigned it are

---

[1] See Postan, op. cit., pp. 215-29, for estimates of the extent of public
ownership.
[2] N. Birnbaum, 'The Crisis in Marxist Sociology', *Social Research*, 1968.
[3] T. H. Marshall, *Citizenship and Social Class*. Cambridge (1950).
[4] K. Galbraith, *The Affluent Society*. London (1958).

implicit in the foregoing account. Let me render them explicit. Instead of simplification and polarization of the division of labour capitalism has produced elaboration and a hierarchy of grades as indicated by Routh (Table Three). The hierarchy of income, educational and prestige levels which these grades represent is a more significant source of social cleavage than that between property owners and the propertyless. Associated with the grades are differences in styles of life, attitudes and values, and discontinuities in social relations. At the same time the hierarchy is also a source of cohesion in so far as it is generally accepted as a reasonably just ordering of things. The various grades compete for income, the lower to some extent emulate the higher, and individuals compete with each other to improve their positions or their children's in the hierarchy. With in addition mass poverty annulled and a more equitable distribution of income now achieved, it is more profitable for an understanding of stratification in our society to treat it in terms of social status than in terms of class.[1] If that is accepted, a diminution of class consciousness is easily accounted for. In general, people are more concerned with social status than with class antagonism. Moreover class conflict has been domesticated through the separation of political and industrial conflict into different institutional channels,[2] Parliament on the one hand and trade unions and employers associations on the other, and through representatives of the working class being able to achieve positions of power, whether as MPs, labour leaders, or on the boards of nationalized industries. In short the working class has been integrated into society, a society in which the former sharp distinctions between capital and labour, state and economic system, ruling class and oppressed class, have lost the clear outlines they formerly had.

While some sociologists, about the turn of the century, were devising new concepts of stratification more suitable than Marx's (they held) for the analysis of modern society,[3] some political theorists were propounding as an explicit counter to Marxism the theory of elites.[4] That the political changes sketched above did take place raises questions about the validity of the concept of a ruling class. Why did they jeopardize their position by extending the franchise? Does not universal adult suffrage separate, in principle, economic and political power? Early elite theorists proposed that the concept of a ruling class fails to describe or explain the power situation in any society and is par-

[1] Marshall, op. cit. See also T. Geiger, *Die Klassengesellschaft im Schmeltztiegel.* Cologne (1949).

[2] The main theme of Dahrendorf, *Class and Class Conflict in Industrial Society.* London (1959).

[3] See M. Abrams, 'Some Measures of Social Stratification in Britain', *Social Stratification*, ed. J. A. Jackson. Cambridge (1968), pp. 113–14.

[4] Useful introductions with references are T. B. Bottomore, *Elites and Society.* Penguin (1966). G. Parry, *Political Elites.* Allen and Unwin (1969).

G

ticularly misleading as regards our own. Ownership of the means of production does not confer political power on owners, on the contrary those who can attain positions of political power will use power as a means to acquire wealth and whatever else is valued in society. The elite are the few who make or influence decisions which decide the fate of the masses, and they may include not only members of a government but also labour leaders and industrialists, and in some versions of the theory, top civil servants and leading military chiefs. They do not rule as representatives of a class, and the ideologies such as representative democracy, by which they secure the acquiescence of the masses to their rule, are not refractions of a structure of relations of production but political formulas consciously conceived to deceive the masses. As against the notion of class conflict, elitists stress the passivity of the masses. They differ in their views as to how elites are recruited and as to whether there is any one self conscious, coherent and closely organized elite or whether there are several representing different interests (industrial, military, etc.) and competing among themselves on any issue, each to promote its particular interest. The most widely known modern versions of the theory are those of J. Burnham[1] and C. W. Mills,[2] both of whom, to some extent, incorporate into it features of Marxist theory. Burnham proposed that the elite in modern society is composed of the managers, particularly managers of industrial organizations. Mills proposed that the modern elite is composed of the most powerful government officials, directors of industry, and military chiefs.

Ideas in the region of elite theory are much favoured by those who consider that our society has moved into a post-capitalist phase, however delineated. The most explicit attempts at its delineation are usually guided by a concept of industrial society. There is of course no one set of ideas to which all delineators subscribe, but there is marked agreement on some of the main ones, stated most boldly by Kerr et al.[3] in their theory of the logic of industrialism. 'Industrializing countries' they assert

'are more nearly like each other, however varied they may be, than they are like commercial or agricultural or hunting or fishing economies'. A central trait of all of them is 'the inevitable and eternal separation of industrial men into managers and managed'.[4]

Another is increasing affluence and well being for all. They recognize that there are still major differences in organization among them, but these can be explained by reference to the past, to the kind of

[1] J. Burnham, *The Managerial Revolution*. Putnam (1942).
[2] C. Wright Mills, *The Power Elite*. OUP (1956).
[3] C. Kerr et al., *Industrialism and Industrial Man*. Heinemann (1962). See also R. Aron, op. cit., and R. Aron, *La Lutte des Classes*. Paris (1964).
[4] Both quotations are from Kerr et al., op. cit., p. 15.

industrializing elite initiating and controlling the process. Such elites may be drawn from members of a traditional landed or military aristocracy as in Japan, revolutionary intellectuals as in Russia, a middle class as in Britain or France, or colonial administrators or nationalist leaders as in much of the third world at the moment. Capitalist society as analysed by Marx is in this view simply an early phase in the industrializing process associated with bourgeois dominance in political affairs, a situation by no means typical in the history of all industrial societies. However, as the various countries enter into the advanced stages of industrialization their social systems tend to converge on a single common type. There is a logic of industrialism forcing all to converge on this type.

At the heart of the logic are requirements inherent in modern methods of production and distribution. Aron remarks that the high rate of investment needed to keep production going requires that surplus value be extracted from the working force whether in a capitalist or a communist society, and decisions made as to where and in what quantity it is to be invested. The decisions will always be made by the managers.[1] The only difference between Western and communist societies in this regard is that in the latter these decisions are part of a national, government-framed plan, but not in the former. Kerr et al. stress rather science and technology as imposing uniform requirements on social organization. A productive system based on them changes constantly in methods and requires a highly skilled, professional and mobile labour force. Positions in it have to be open to acquisition by the most skilled, hence

'industrialism . . . is against tradition and status based upon family, class, religion, race of caste'.[2]

Accordingly rates of social mobility have to be high, and rewards, of income and social status, to be distributed according to levels of skill. Local customs and cultures, sectarian ideologies, are destroyed as science and large scale organization impose uniformities in ideas, activities and schedules. There is general consensus among the whole population on the value of production and economic growth, on science, education, mobility and achievement, and on the principle by which rewards are distributed. Government accordingly, in the hands of an omnipresent state, is merely a matter of adjudicating among the claims of competing interest groups. These all agree on a basic web of rules which regulate competition and methods of dispute settlement, and permit a degree of democratic control over the provision of general welfare. Managers now in command of the productive system have

[1] R. Aron, *Eighteen Lectures on Industrial Society*. London (1967), chap. 5.
[2] Kerr *et al.*, op. cit., p. 35.

interests quite different from those of early capitalists or their heirs. They are interested above all in keeping production going, indeed in expanding it, in innovation, in expertise regardless of social origins, and prefer their own authority to be based on consensus and not the power to dismiss. In this climate, ideologies of conflict wither and die.[1] Through the application of science and technology to industry the contribution of labour as sheer human energy to the productive process diminishes. According to a recent estimate twenty-nine per cent of the gross national product of the USA is derived from 'the knowledge industry'.[2] This to some gives hope that Marx's forecast of the abolition of labour can eventually be realized.[3] Theorists of industrial society are more concerned with the present implications of the process. They claim that in the more technologically advanced installations many of the operatives, as where they monitor automatic production systems for example, are hardly distinguishable in pay and conditions of work from management.[4] Moreover the same web of rules governs the daily activities of both management and operatives. This, together with the more satisfying nature of the work and frequent consultative interaction between managers and operatives has not only ended alienation but encouraged workers to identify with the enterprise.[5]

As well as by consensus and high rates of mobility, stratification in industrial society is characterized by a decreasing degree of differentiation between strata and by increasing consistency among the various dimensions of stratification.[6] By decreasing differentiation is meant that the gap or range separating top and bottom of the scale is increasingly reduced, and that the majority of the population come to occupy positions in the middle ranges of the system. In an influential paper K. Mayer showed that by the early fifties in the USA the group with incomes between $4,000 and $7,000 per year had grown from 15·1 per cent in 1910 to 34·9 per cent in 1954, and that over half the group were manual workers. Further, 37 per cent of families with after-tax incomes of $7,500 were headed by manual workers.[7] Evidence that higher-paid manual workers were earning more than lower-paid

[1] See R. Bendix, *Work and Authority in Industry*. N.Y. (1965). J. K. Galbraith, *The New Industrial State*. London (1967). D. Bell, *The End of Ideology*. Free Press (1960).

[2] F. Mackluh, *The Production and Distribution of Knowledge in the United States*. Priceton (1962).

[3] See for example H. Marcuse, *One-Dimensional Man*. Routledge (1964), pp. 42–6.

[4] See for example Postan, op. cit., pp. 320–6. Galbraith, op. cit., chaps 23 and 24.   [5] R. Blauner, *Alienation and Freedom*. Chicago (1964).

[6] A notable critique of these ideas is given by J. Goldthorpe, 'Social Stratification in Industrial Society', *The Sociological Review Monograph*, no. 8, October 1964.

[7] K. Mayer, 'Recent Changes in the Class Structure of the United States', *Transactions of the Third World Congress of Sociology*, vol. 3, 1956.

non-manual workers was also forthcoming from Britain and Europe.[1]

Mayer argued that manual workers were also attaining levels of education and material comfort equivalent to those of the non-manual. The notion that we are becoming a middle class society, that middle class values are the dominant ones and are accepted as standards both by the elite and by labourers, is usually present, explicitly or implicitly, in the writings of industrial society theorists. Some authors have seen in this alleged disappearance of differentials between manual and lower-paid non-manual workers a reversal of Marx's prediction that the majority of the population would be reduced to proletariat.[2] It is certainly not that. The vast majority of non-manual workers are proletariat in Marx's sense. What is happening, if it is correct that differentials are disappearing between those two sectors, is that two status groups are merging, or two classes in Weber's sense of income classes. By increasing consistency is meant that previously separate dimensions of stratification merge, so that an individuals' position in one is the same as his position in another.[3] The *nouveau riche*, the poor scholar and the impoverished man of rank disappear from the social scene. Consistency increases because rewards have to be distributed in accordance with performance in the occupational sphere, which performance is to a considerable extent correlated with level of education. The derivation of much of this theory from, or its consistency with, Parsons' functionalism is obvious. Two points should be noted. First, industrial society theorists disagree among themselves particularly concerning the relation between state and society. Some, referring to the relation in the USSR, maintain that there is no necessary connection between industrial society and democratic government.[4] Second, many Marxist commentators agree with the general picture of industrial society presented in these writings, its growing affluence, decreasing differentials between grades of labour, domestication of class conflict, and levelling of styles of life. They add, however, that we are still alienated, estranged from our true potentialities by the nature of industrial work and organization, and by the world view imposed on us by the mass media and liberal education.[5] The matter is discussed below.

British sociologists have been less concerned than continental and American to develop theories of industrial society and its system of

---

[1] See Transactions, vol. 3. D. Lockwood, *The Black Coated Worker*. London (1966).

[2] Mayer, op. cit., p. 78. J. Bernard, 'Class Organization in an Era of Abundance', *Transactions of the Third World Society*, vol. 3, 1956.

[3] On this subject see G. E. Lenski, 'Status Crystallization: A Non-Vertical Dimension of Social Status', *A.S.R.*, vol. 19, 1954.

[4] See for example A. Bauer, *et al.*, *How the Soviet System Works*, Princeton (1956).

[5] Marcuse, op. cit.

stratification. Their contributions have been mostly towards distributional studies or aspects of stratification in a local context. One major British contribution, however, has been towards discussion of the thesis of embourgeoisement present explicitly or implicitly in industrial society theory, i.e. the thesis that the manual working class has not simply been integrated into society but is being incorporated into the lower sections of the middle non-manual class. Before turning to discuss some of the main ideas presented above, consider the conceptions of class found in sociological writings.

Class in current research

Study of stratification involves inquiries in its three dimensions and in various problem areas. There is, for example, the area comprising questions about distributions of property, income, social status or life chances; the area of questions about the distribution of population among classes and rates of mobility between them; and the area concerned with relations between classes, personal relationships between members of different classes or status groups and differences in life style or culture between them. Given these problem areas, that sociologists are bound to be variously interested in them, and that they differ in their views as to the relative significance of the three dimensions of stratification, it is not surprising that the term class is used with varying denotations in current literature.

It is of course not necessary, in order to contribute to our understanding of stratification, to select a class or several classes as the object of study. What one takes as the object of study should depend upon the question to which one seeks an answer. If one wants to know, for example, whether or not the better off members of the working class are being assimilated into the middle class, one should select a population of such workers and find out if they are accepted as friends by middle class people, if their life style is the same and so on. This is what the team conducting the enquiry into the affluent worker did.[1] Studies of distributions in particular can provide valuable information without being directly concerned with social classes. Here for example is an extremely informative Table of distributions of private capital in which the classes are purely nominal, not social.

The table indicates that (taking the value of the £ as having halved between the two periods considered) in the earlier period 2 per cent of property owners owned among them 66 per cent of all private capital, and in the later period 1·5 per cent owned 54 per cent. Although during the later period a Labour Government was in power, the redistribution of property occurring then, the authors remark, 'has not been of striking proportions'.

For reasons indicated above, until recently British and American

[1] Goldthorpe *et al.*, op. cit., chap. 2.

TABLE FOUR

Distribution of private capital in Great Britain, 1936–38 and 1946–50*

Size of holding	1936–38				1946–50			
	Number (thousands)	per cent	value (£ million)	per cent	number (thousands)	per cent	value (£ million)	per cent
Under £100	21,421	75·5	1,015	5·3	19,633	62·4	883	3·0
£100	4,983	17·6	2,208	11·4	8,448	26·8	3,479	11·6
£1,000	1,436	5·1	3,348	17·3	2,389	7·6	5,607	18·7
£5,000	253	0·9	1,931	10·0	510	1·6	3,854	12·9
£10,000	172	0·6	2,813	14·6	338	1·1	5,453	18·2
£25,000	77	0·3	3,094	19·1	137	0·4	6,229	20·8
£100,000	15	0·1	4,304	22·3	19	0·06	4,402	14·7
Total	28,356	100·0	19,313	100·0	31,474	100·0	29,907	100·0

* Taken from A. M. Carr-Saunders et al., Social Conditions in England and Wales. Oxford (1958), p. 176.

research has been guided more by concepts of status than of class, status in this sense meaning simply prestige, not a bundle of legal rights or disabilities. Also sociologists have, especially since the war, paid more attention than hitherto to the subjective aspects of stratification, to ascertaining people's ideas as to what our system of stratification is, their assessments of their various positions in it, and their attitudes to these. To some extent this shift in attention follows logically upon the decision to explore the dimension of status, for to do so thoroughly one must find out what or who people regard as prestigious and to what degree. There were probably other reasons for the shift, having to do with, in Britain at least, the general intellectual climate of the post-war years, dominated by logical positivism, a style which hardly encourages the investigation of society by way of conceptual structures which seem, as in some versions of Marxism, to be assigned an existence independent of and more powerful than that of the individual.[1] Whatever the reasons, research focused more sharply on the individual. The raw material of research became the response of the individual to questionnaires, his remarks during interviews, or such routines of his conduct as the participant-observer managed to catch a glimpse of. Marx wrote:

'It is not a question of knowing what this or that proletarian, or even the proletariat as a whole, *conceives* as its aims at any particular moment. It is a question of knowing *what* the proletariat *is*, and what it must historically accomplish in its *nature*. Its aims and its historical activity are ordained for it, in a tangible and irrevocable way, by its own situation as well as by the whole organization of present day society.'[2]

However, given the focus and techniques mentioned it becomes precisely a question of knowing, figuratively speaking, what this or that proletarian conceives as his aims. Classes now tend to be thought of as each a number of individuals exhibiting common characteristics, or to put it another way, variations in rewards, material or social, in life chances, aims and ideas are regarded not so much as symptomatic of variations in position in, and response to, the exigencies of an underlying remote or deep structure, but as representative of classes of persons variously rewarded, having such and such ideas and aims.

One result to emerge from asking people what their conceptions of our system of stratification are, or what their images of society are,[3] is that there is no general agreement as to the nature of the system.

---

[1] A typical product of that climate is K. Popper, *The Open Society and its Enemies*. London (1952).

[2] In *The Holy Family*, quoted by R. Blackburn, 'The Unequal Society', *New Left Review*, 1967.

[3] A. Willener, *Images de la Société et Classes Sociales*. Bern (1957).

People's images vary, though as we shall see below, the variations mostly cluster round a few general types. One possible way of interpreting this fact is to adopt a strictly Durkheimian attitude to these images, to view them as symbols expressing social relationships. The most extreme statement of this view is Bott's:

'People do have direct experience of distinctions of power and prestige in their places of work, among their colleagues, in schools, and in their relationships with friends, neighbours and relatives. In other words the ingredients, the raw materials of class ideology are located in the individual's various primary social experiences, rather than in his position in a socio-economic category. The hypothesis advanced here is that when an individual talks about class he is trying to say something, in a symbolic form, about his experiences of power and prestige in his actual membership groups and social relationships both past and present.'[1]

Class in this view is treated as a collective representation, a way of communicating experience of primary relationships which alters its configuration with alterations in such experience, as the totem in an Australian tribe changes from kangaroo to eaglehawk from one clan to another.

It hardly needs saying that in the last few years there has been a revival of interest in Marxism among European sociologists. Accordingly in current sociology various conceptions of class are in use, class as an abstract economic function, as a collection of individuals sharing a common place in a hierarchy of social prestige or in the division of labour, and class as a collective representation.

In most research, classes on a national level are identified by reference to broad types of occupations, as in the Registrar General's division of the population into five social classes ranked according to the general standing within the community of the occupations concerned. The classes and the proportions of the working population in each are shown for 1951 in the following table (Table 5).

Moser and Hall tried to meet an objection often made against the Registrar General's scheme, viz. that we do not know if the community agrees with his evaluation of the standing of occupations, by a somewhat complicated procedure. They first themselves ranked thirty occupations and then asked some members of the community to rank the same thirty into five grades, and finally to rank occupations within each grade. Table Six shows the distributions of respondents' votes evaluating the standing of the occupations, from grade A to E.

Moser and Hall claim that respondents' rankings agree with their

---

[1] E. Bott, *Family and Social Network*. London (1957), p. 163.

TABLE FIVE

Social class	Occupational type	Number in thousands	Percentage of total population
1 Upper and middle	Higher professional and directors of large businesses	510·3	3·31
2 Intermediate	Lower professional owners and managers of small businesses, farmers	2,243·0	14·54
3 Skilled workers and clerical workers	Artisans, clerks, foremen, supervisors	8,160·8	52·89
4 Intermediate	Semiskilled workers, agricultural workers	2,490·0	16·4
5 Unskilled workers	Labourers	2,024·6	13·12

TABLE SIX

Percentage of sample placing occupations into each of the five initial grades*

Occupation	A	B	C	D	E
Medical Officer of Health	89	10	1	—	—
Company director	87	12	1	—	—
Country solicitor	74	24	2	—	—
Chartered accountant	66	31	3	—	—
Civil servant (executive grade)	34	53	12	1	—
Nonconformist Minister	32	54	12	2	—
Business manager	28	62	10	—	—
Works manager	28	59	12	1	—
Farmer	21	58	19	2	—
Elementary school teacher	3	38	54	5	—
Jobbing master builder	2	35	54	9	—
News reporter	2	33	58	7	—
Commercial traveller	1	23	61	14	1
Chef	1	21	56	21	1
Insurance agent	—	13	60	25	2
Newsagent and tobacconist	—	10	59	29	2
Policeman	1	8	55	34	2
Routine clerk	—	6	54	37	3
Fitter	—	6	43	44	2
Carpenter	—	3	34	59	4
Shop assistant	—	1	27	62	10
Bricklayer	—	2	19	61	18
Tractor driver	—	1	10	58	31
Coal hewer	—	2	10	44	44
Railway porter	—	—	3	30	67
Barman	—	—	2	29	69
Agricultural labourer	—	1	5	23	71
Carter	—	—	2	14	84
Road sweeper	—	—	1	4	95

* From ed. D. V. Glass, *Social Mobility in Britain*. London (1954), p. 39.

own. It is, however, difficult to know what they mean by this when it is clear that the respondents did not agree with each other. About the most one can say is that, somewhat analogously to the caste system, there is general agreement regarding rankings in the region of top and bottom and little agreement about the middle ones. Moser and Hall disarmingly mention a major drawback to their own and similar schemes, namely that we cannot tell what the significance is, if indeed there is any, of the supposed discontinuities between grades. Do chartered accountants refuse to let their daughters marry a civil servant (executive grade), do they vote differently and have different life styles ? We do not know, but it seems unlikely. In fact many of the researches referred to below indicate that a major discontinuity is that between manual and non-manual workers, a distinction ignored in these schemes, though the Registrar General has recently incorporated it into a scheme of classification. Oldman and Illsley point out that rating procedures which involve forced-choice replies are bound to produce stereotyped answers when people may in fact be indifferent to the question.[1] The value of these schemes for at least some kinds of longitudinal studies has recently been questioned. J. W. B. Douglas, in the course of enquiries involved in following the medical and educational experiences of a national sample of children, found that manual workers change occupations frequently, especially from semiskilled to skilled occupations or vice versa,

'and so even the Registrar General's classification . . . would turn out to be fluctuating and impermanent. . . .'[2]

Recently F. Parkin has pointed out that we cannot infer, from the rankings obtained by such procedures as Moser and Hall used, that people morally approve of these rankings; these may simply be their perception of an existing state of affairs, or of what they take to be the general opinion on the matter.[3] In fact we know from other studies that some people do not agree with the Registrar General's and similar rankings.

'A sizeable minority of men in Bethnal Green take a very different view from white collar people about the status of manual work, placing jobs such as company directors and chartered accountants towards the bottom of the scale and manual jobs, like agricultural labourer, coal miner, and bricklayer, towards the top.'[4]

[1] D. Oldman and R. Illsley, 'Measuring the Status of Occupations', *Sociological Review*, no. 14, 1966.
[2] J. W. B. Douglas, *The Home and The School*. London (1964), p. 40.
[3] F. Parkin, *Class, Inequality and Political Order*. London (1971).
[4] M. Young and P. Willmott, *Family and Kinship in East London*. Penguin (1972), p. 29.

These white collar occupations, they felt, were not so functionally necessary to the productive system as the manual ones.

Despite the many criticisms levelled against these schemes much useful research has been done using them. The Registrar General's scheme has been extensively used, for example, in social medicine. However, most sociologists now consider it essential to distinguish, in the Registrar General's class 3, between manual and non-manual workers, some arguing that the major line of cleavage falls between these two occupational categories. The reason for this view is not simply that discontinuities in social relationships, norms of behaviour and attitudes at this point have been reported in numerous studies (see page 142), or that commercial or market research firms find it useful to distinguish between the two,[1] even though the other classes in their scheme are delimited solely by income level, presumably because there are significant differences in consumption patterns between them. More significantly, the two categories differ in class position in that their work situations[2] and total rewards differ, even though the majority in both are propertyless and even though some manual workers earn more than some non-manual. White collar workers are closer to managers in conditions and type of work than are manual workers, and their chances of promotion to that level much higher. In most industrial installations the division between staff and worker is basic, and manual workers habitually identify white collar workers as staff, however humble the positions the latter may occupy. A recent German study reports that manual workers consider that white collar workers do not work, in what they take to be the only valid meaning of the word.[3] Certainly non-manual work is rarely dangerous or physically damaging through noise or heat, dust or dirt, or sheer arduousness. As regards rewards, even though starting salaries for non-manual workers in many areas are below the earnings of some or many manual workers, the former mostly enjoy greater security of tenure and higher and more regular increments in rewards so that their salaries in time exceed those of the latter. They more often enjoy benefits not always available to the latter. A recent survey finds that among the firms examined 43 per cent had no sick pay scheme for manual workers while over 90 per cent of the white collar force were covered by such schemes. Many firms had no pensions scheme for the manual workers while almost all had for the non-manual. The latter also have longer paid holidays, and are less subject to penalties for being late at work.[4]

At the same time one cannot treat these categories as two bounded groups, each internally homogeneous and absolutely separate from

---

[1] D. Marsh, op. cit., p. 206.
[2] Lockwood, op. cit.
[3] R. Popitz et al., *Das Gesellschaftsbild des Arbeiters*, Tübingen (1957).
[4] D. Wedderburn and C. Craig, cited in Parkin, op. cit., p. 25.

each other. First, there are differences in class position in the above sense and in status between various sections within the manual population. Craftsmen, for example, are much more advantageously placed in the labour market than are unskilled labourers, while a recurrent theme in studies of working class life is that of the status distinction between roughs and respectables. The former spend in a feckless sort of way, refusing to plan expenditure for a possible future, and borrow and lend among themselves. The respectables withdraw from too intimate an association with neighbours, value independence and often aspire to move into the middle class. Second, several researchers report the existence of a sunken middle class whose circumstances and life style include features of those of both categories. Thus:

'These were all manual workers' homes: yet manifestly this did not always fit either with the bountiful display of material possessions, or more importantly with their whole style of living. Six of the fathers had once owned their own small business and had turned to their present manual work when that collapsed.'[1]

In short, the hierarchy of occupational categories exhibits no sharp discontinuities. This means that differences between categories must be expressed statistically, or in terms of ideal types, or by some combination of these techniques.[2] Accepting that the manual/non-manual distinction is at least of considerable importance, the hierarchy is:

Professional, managerial and administrative
Semiprofessional and lower administrative
Routine white collar
Skilled manual
Semiskilled manual
Unskilled manual

Like all such schemes, this one embodies elements of both class and status as criteria of differentiation.

The kind of social status dealt with in local community studies is perhaps analytically purer, and local systems of stratification are apt to differ in some respects from these national models. The methods used in these studies have been described above (see pages 32–34). Briefly, a man's status is determined by his acceptability as an associate with others of equal status in contexts outside of work. His social network of friends and relatives are for the most part of the same status as himself. Thus Williams found in Gosforth seven local status groups or aggregates, some distinguished by criteria not taken account of in

[1] B. Jackson and D. Marsden, *Education and the Working Class*. London (1962), p. 53. See also Douglas, op. cit., chap. 6; and Goldthorpe *et al.*, op. cit., pp. 94–6.
[2] See for example Goldthorpe *et al.*, op. cit., chap. 5.

the national models. For example, the differences between the top and second top strata is not one of wealth or occupation, but that members of the former behave like gentlemen while the latter do not. Or, the roughs at the bottom were distinguished from the stratum above purely by life style, not occupation.[1]

Some sociologists consider that studies of local stratification systems contribute little to our understanding of the subject, for a variety of reasons. (a) Local communities differ in the kind of populations composing them (mining villages, rural parishes, schools, housing estates, etc.), so that local systems differ accordingly. Moreover in none, or few, is the class distribution of population similar to that of the nation, so that none or few can be taken as representative of the nation in that respect. (b) Even if the class composition (by for instance the Registrar General's scheme) of a community should be similar to that of the notion, one cannot within any one community study the operations of those institutional complexes, the market, Parliament, or the educational system for example, which are the real sources of unequal distributions of income, property or whatever. Studies of local status systems merely codify the banal snobberies of quotidian existence, and the conception of status employed in them is a trivialization of what Weber had in mind by the term, exemplified in the last two Chapters. The only groups in our society with a specific status at all resembling that of castes or slaves are coloured and perhaps other immigrants, or Catholics in Ulster.[2] (c) In any case, the larger and more occupationally varied the community the less likely is there to be agreement amongst its members as to what the local status system is. For example, after close study of Banbury (population 19,000), Margaret Stacey concluded that:

> 'It is not possible to construct for Banbury and district a simple n-fold class system. That is to say, the total population cannot be placed in a series of horizontal groupings, members of each group being assumed to have parity with each other and able to recognize each other as social equals if they should meet. Nor is it possible to place people upon one social status scale, ranked on a basis of commonly agreed social characteristics.'[3]

The reason why it is not possible is because of a major cleavage of the population between locals and cosmopolitans. Locals are those oriented to the local traditional social system, while cosmopolitans are those who, while having to work and live in Banbury, ignore the local system

---

[1] W. M. Williams, *The Sociology of an English Village: Gosforth*. London (1956). See also J. Littlejohn, *Westrigg, the Sociology of a Cheviot Parish*. London (1963).

[2] This view is forcefully argued by Parkin, op. cit.

[3] M. Stacey, *Tradition and Change*. OUP (1960), p. 144.

and derive their social frame of reference from organizations and opportunities beyond it. Locals consider that the top status group is composed of families who for generations have been dominant land-owners prominent in local government. To the cosmopolitans the top group is epitomized in the person of a self made man now chairman of several engineering companies; he seldom resides in his local hall and plays no part in local affairs. A typical working class local accepts the local status system as reasonably just, votes Conservative and does not belong to a trade union. His cosmopolitan equivalent belongs to a union and votes Labour, considers that the local status system is non-sense and that society is divided simply into bosses and workers. The middle class local typically owns a small family business, considers public service a duty and is Anglican and Tory. Like his father before him he intends to live and die in Banbury, endowing his son with the business. His cosmopolitan equivalent has a degree from a provincial university and is liable to be a technologist or manager. He is not much interested in religion but joins local sports clubs. His main interest is his own career and he is ready to leave Banbury to promote it. A some-what similar split amongst the middle class in local communities has been observed by W. Watson, who called the two types burgesses and spiralists.[1] Subsequent studies have shown that not only do the careers and social activities of the heads of families within each differ but that family organization differs also.[2] Accordingly, insofar as these are features of life styles, it would seem that life styles may vary con-siderably within one status group.

Such objections to studies of local systems are acceptable, but they serve to circumscribe their limitations, not to invalidate them. We cannot ignore the local community, for example, in any consideration of the process of socialization whereby people accept or adapt to the national system of stratification. For most children the family, the neighbourhood and the local school are the main socializing agencies, while there is some evidence (see page 136) that people's images of society are conditioned to some extent by the kind of community they inhabit. As Birnbaum remarks:

'Contemporary elites seem able to obtain legitimation, or at least tacit acquiescence in their elite status, from contemporary popula-tions simply by allowing the constraints of economic necessity, familial obligation and community membership, to take effect',[3]

[1] W. Watson, 'Social Mobility and Social Class in Industrial Communities', *Closed Systems and Open Minds*, eds M. Gluckman and E. Devons. Edinburgh (1964).
[2] C. Bell, *Middle Class Families*. London (1968).
[3] N. Birnbaum, 'The Idea of Industrial Society', *Sociological Review Monograph*, no. 8, 1964, p. 7.

adding that the version of society propagated by the mass media reinforces daily experience.

Finally, I stress again that stratification exhibits different facets in different contexts, and the populations to be considered as strata should in any instance be those from study of which one can best throw light on the problem under consideration. Douglas for example in the study mentioned above found that the best way of making sense of data relating children's performace in examinations to their home backgrounds was to divide non-manual and manual workers' families each into two groups, according to the educational experience of the parents.[1] Whether the four classes so obtained are status aggregates or not is of no importance whatsoever.

Equality and inequality in modern society

It is now appropriate to consider the themes raised at the beginning of the previous Chapter, particularly the argument that inequalities in the distribution of wealth and income have been diminishing as a result of processes inherent in the latest phase of capitalist society. Some authors consider that industrial society by its nature ensures a more equitable distribution than agrarian society. Lenski argues this, citing as evidence that the disparity in income between the richest and poorest at present is less than that between medieval king or Roman emperor and the poorest serfs or slaves.[2] The comparison, however, is invalid since the king's and emperor's private fortune was not distinguished from the state treasury. They had to finance public works and pay armies and civil servants from it. Moreover, because of the nature of the productive systems then, scope for profitable investments were much more limited than now. It is doubtful if the disparity, in these crude terms, is any the less. In any case, in considering the question in modern society we must distinguish between property and income.

Various estimates have been made of the current distribution in the UK of private property or wealth, and of changes in its distribution this century. Bottomore cites that from 1911–13 1 per cent of the population owned 68 per cent of all private property; in 1946–7 1 per cent still owned 50 per cent of private property.[3] Westergaard states that in 1955 1 per cent of the population owned 40 per cent of private property, and 10 per cent of the population owned 80 per cent of it.[4] Blackburn states that the richest 7 per cent of the population own

---

[1] Douglas, op. cit., pp. 44–5.
[2] G. E. Lenski, op. cit.
[3] T. B. Bottomore, *Classes in Modern Society*. Allen and Unwin (1965), p. 34.
[4] J. H. Westergaard, 'Capitalism without Classes?', *New Left Review*, no. 26, 1964, pp. 10–34.

84 per cent of all private wealth while the richest 2 per cent own
55 per cent.[1] A recent survey claims that 1 per cent of the population
own 20 per cent of the personal wealth, 9 per cent own one half, and
25 per cent own three-quarters.[2] Clearly, unless one is prepared to do
a great deal of work towards understanding the methods by which
these figures were arrived at, the definitions of property or personal
wealth used, etc., one has no reason to prefer one set to another.
However, it can hardly be denied that all indicate a massive inequality
in the distribution of property such that, it seems to me, there is no
reason not to continue to speak of capitalist society, whetever changes
have occured over the last century.

Shareholding of the more profitable type would seem to be even
more concentrated than ownership of other types of property. 'Only
4 per cent of the adult population hold any shares in commercial
or industrial companies, according to a recent stock exchange survey'.[3]
Figures from America on this point confirm the broad picture. A
Brookings Institute study of 1957 covering 2,991 major corporations
discovered that 2·1 per cent of the common stock shareholdings
owned 58 per cent of the common stock and that 1·1 per cent of the
preferred stockholdings owned 40 per cent of the preferred stock; in
1953 the 9 per cent of the population at the top of the income groupings
owned more than 46 per cent of the nation's net private assets.[4]

Turning now to income, it seems that during this century the share
of the national income accruing to property has diminished relative
to income from employment.[5] Feinstein summarizes a variety of
calculations for the UK in the following table.

As with all macroeconomic calculations one has to be aware, before
accepting these figures as indicating anything more than a general
trend, that different methods produce different results.[6] Does one
include professional people's earnings under the heading of labour, or
not? How does one calculate the relative share of income from employment and property in the case of the self employed? The percentage
of professional people who are employers or self employed has steadily
decreased from 34 per cent in 1931 to 18 per cent in 1951, or to 13 per
cent if doctors are regarded as employees of the Ministry of Health.[7]

[1] Blackburn, op. cit. A major source for estimates of distributions of property
and income is J. E. Meade, *Efficiency, Equality and the Ownership of Property*.
London (1964).
[2] M. Forsyth, *Property and Property Distribution*. P.E.P. Research Publications, London (1971). Cited in *New Society*, 26 August 1971.
[3] Blackburn, op. cit.
[4] G. Kolko, *Wealth and Power in America*. N.Y. (1962).
[5] Eds. J. Marchal and D. Ducros, *The Distribution of National Income*.
Macmillan (1968).
[6] See the discussion following Feinstein's paper, ibid.
[7] G. Routh, op. cit. (229), p. 16.

H

TABLE SEVEN

The distribution of net domestic income for the UK excluding rent on dwellings between labour and property*

Years	Labour	Property
	percent of net domestic income	
1910–14	68·8	31·2
1921–24	79·8	20·2
1925–29	79·9	20·1
1930–34	81·7	18·3
1935–38	80·3	19·7
1946–49	82·4	17·6
1950–54	82·0	18·0
1956–59	83·5	16·5
1960–63	84·0	16·0

* C. H. Feinstein, ibid., p. 128.

How are we to take account of such facts in making the relevant calculations? By some calculations it would appear that labour's share of the national income (presumably including rents and profits on non-domestic property) relative to property has not greatly increased, if at all, during this century.[1] Doubtless the relative share of each varies over different short-run periods. John Hughes estimates that over the decade 1955–65 personal property income has been rising proportionately faster than earned income, as shown in the following Table.

TABLE EIGHT

Personal property income and earned income 1955–65*

	1955	1960	1965
	£ million	£ million	£ million
Personal property income	1,534	2,372	3,595
Earned income	12,905	17,168	23,736
	Indices (1955 = 100)		
Personal property income	100	155	234
Earned income	100	133	184

* J. Hughes, 'The Increase in Inequality', New Statesman, 8 November, 1968.

In general, the redistribution of factor incomes does not seem to have been of striking proportions.

Calculation of the distribution of personal incomes is also difficult. However the author of the most authoritative recent survey of changes in types and amounts of pay between 1906 and 1960 concludes that

[1] Blackburn, op. cit.

'the outstanding characteristic of the national pay structure is the rigidity of its relationships';[1]

pay differentials between the various types of occupations remain, as shown in Table Nine.[2]

The table indicates that:

(a) there as been a slight trend towards the lowering of pay in the top ranges and raising of pay in the bottom ranges;

(b) lower professionals have experienced a greater diminution of pay differential than any other class;

(c) clerks average pay has become less than that of the skilled manual class;

(d) managers' pay has risen proportionately higher than that of any other class.

Total income distribution, including income from property, is of course a different matter from pay distribution as calculated from average earnings of occupational classes. According to one assessment of the former, the top 9 per cent of income earners in the UK receive 27 per cent of the total of personal income pre-tax, and 23·6 per cent of it after tax; while the bottom 36·6 per cent of income earners receive 12·95 per cent of the total pre-tax and 14·4 per cent after tax.[3] There is in fact some evidence that inequality as between the top tenth and bottom third is currently increasing, both in the UK and the USA. Kolko calculates that the lowest 50 per cent of income earners in the USA received 27 per cent of the national personal income in 1910 and 23 per cent in 1959, while the share of the richest tenth remained constant over the period and the only significant rises in income distribution have occurred in the second and third richest tenths.[4] Titmuss presents much the same picture of changes in income distribution in Britain.[5] In Britain in 1960, it was estimated, about 18 per cent of households (some 7·5 million people) were living below a defined national assistance level of living, and in the USA rather more.

Since personal income distribution has to be estimated from tax returns, the extent of the disparity between richest and poorest is greater than available figures suggest, for a proportion of income of the former accrues to them in the form of life assurances, superannuation, capital gains, expense accounts and other fringe benefits. Meade judges that personal income from property, as estimated from tax returns, may be underestimated by as much as £1,500 million. Taxation, at least in

[1] Routh, op. cit., p. 147.
[2] Ibid., p. 104.
[3] National Income and Expenditure. HMSO (1966).
[4] Kolko, op. cit. See also H. P. Miller, Rich Man, Poor Man. N.Y. (1964).
[5] R. M. Titmuss, Income Distribution and Social Change. London (1962).

TABLE NINE

Average earnings of men in seven occupational classes 1913–1960

Occupation	1913–14 £	1922–24 £	as percentage of 1913–14	1935–36 £	as percentage of 1922–24	1955–56 £	as percentage of 1935–36	1960 £	as percentage of 1955–56	as percentage of 1913–14
1 Professional										
A Higher	328	582	(177)	634	(109)	1,541	(243)	2,034	(132)	620
B Lower	155	320	(206)	308	(96)	610	(198)	847	(139)	546
2 Managers, etc.	200	480	(240)	440	(92)	1,480	(336)	1,850	(125)	925
3 Clerks	99	182	(184)	192	(105)	523	(272)	682	(130)	689
4 Foremen	113	268	(237)	273	(102)	784	(287)	1,015	(129)	898
5 Skilled manual	99	180	(181)	195	(108)	622	(319)	796	(128)	804
6 Semiskilled manual	69	126	(183)	134	(106)	469	(350)	581	(124)	842
7 Unskilled	63	128	(203)	129	(101)	435	(337)	535	(123)	849
Averages										
Current weights	92	180	(194)	186	(104)	634	(340)	808	(127)	874
1911 weights	92	177	(191)	185	(104)	590	(319)	746	(126)	807

Britain in the sixties (apart from death duties, a large proportion of which may often be evaded by timely gifts), was not progressive but regressive, i.e. the proportion of income taken in tax increased for lower income households as against higher incomes.[1]

Clearly, while *per capita* income has increased for the vast majority and property income has diminished somewhat relative to employment income, there are good grounds for concluding that

> 'the general advance in the material conditions of the British working class, in recent decades, has been due overwhelmingly to the rapid growth of national income . . . and not to any radical redistribution of wealth or income between classes'.[2]

Probably the main reason for the continuing inequality in distribution of wealth, in the sense of both property owning and income from it, is the increasing concentration of capital in giant firms or immense groupings of firms. In the USA by the sixties the five top industrial corporations held one-eighth of all manufacturing assets; in Britain one hundred and eighty firms employing one-third of the labour force in manufacturing accounted for one half of net capital expenditure in 1963. These giants can afford to provide directly out of profits between 70–80 per cent of the funds they use; the self financing of investment out of profits disproportionately benefits, through growth, the shareholders.[3]

The maintenance of pay differentials between occupational categories is due to a variety of processes. Some of the professions and crafts control to a greater or lesser degree their intake of new recruits, thus ensuring that their skills are scarce enough to maintain their market value. Maintenance of pay differentials between manual occupations would seem to have become the main task of trade unions. Employers, and especially the giant firms who have to plan their production and marketing operations for several years ahead, are only too anxious to avoid trouble with trade unions, and readily accede to a demand for higher wages, usually with some understanding that the union concerned will then help to keep industrial peace.[4] The increase in production cost is then passed on to the consumer in the form of an increase in the cost of the product. Who the consumers are depends on the product, but with regard to many of the most important, for instance the supply or power to industry, a rise in price results in a rise in price of a wide range of other products, including in the end general con-

---

[1] Hughes, op. cit. The range of household incomes Hughes considers is from £559–£676 to £2,122–£2,566.

[2] Bottomore, op. cit., p. 37.

[3] Figures in this paragraph are taken from M. Kidron, *Western Capitalism since the War*. Penguin (1970), pp. 26–7.

[4] This and many other processes are discussed by Kidron, ibid.

sumer goods. Other unions, under pressure from their members, then demand a wage rise to maintain the value of their members' wage packet at the same relative level as before. Any particular union may obtain for its members, or a section of them, a considerable advantage in the general competition for a short period, but in the long run differentials remain much as they have been since the beginning of the century. Routh was so impressed by this long-term stability that he suggested that the market forces of supply and demand do not determine the price of labour, or at least differential prices of the various kinds of labour, but that instead the determination of differential prices is governed by an implicit concept of a fair wage, understood by workers if not by management. They were so governed, explicitly, in the locally bounded economies of feudal society,[1] and are so governed in the caste system. It is an attractive idea, anathema doubtless to economists. That there have been the changes shown above would seem to indicate that market forces do have some influence on the process.

Life chances

In a somewhat final sense life chances are influenced by class position, in that mortality rates vary among the classes, as shown in Table Ten.

TABLE TEN

Standard mortality ratios for different social classes, standard population, men aged 20–64, England and Wales

Registrar General's social class	1921–23	1943–32	1950
1	82	90	97
2	94	94	86
3	95	97	102
4	101	102	94
5	125	111	118

Until 1930 it was possible to present the variations as a gradient, showing a rise in mortality the lower the class. The picture is slightly more complex now, perhaps for some instances because of changes in the Registrar General's allocation of particular occupations to one or other class. Also differences in mortality rates between classes vary in different age groups. A recent survey of relevant studies concludes that differentials in mortality rates between the middle levels and

---

[1] A. M. Carr-Saunders et al., op. cit., p. 13. The standard mortality ratio is a measure of the difference between deaths in a given class and deaths in the standard population.

class 1 have all but disappeared, but that class 5 is still strikingly worse off compared with the rest.[1]

Infant mortality rates present a slightly different picture of an overall decrease, and of a maintenance of differentials between classes with class 5 still much worse off than the others.

TABLE ELEVEN

Neonatal, post-neonatal, and total infant mortality rates per 1,000 legitimate live births, by social class, England and Wales, 1921, 1939, and 1950[*]

| | | | Social class | | | All |
Age at death, and year	1	2	3	4	5	classes
Neonatal deaths (0–4 weeks)						
1921	23·4	28·3	33·7	36·7	36·9	33·9
1939	18·9	23·4	25·4	27·7	30·1	26·4
1950	12·9	16·2	17·6	19·8	21·9	18·1
(1950 rate as percentage of 1921)	55·1	57·2	52·2	54·0	59·3	53·4
Post-neonatal deaths (4 weeks to 1 year)						
1921	15·0	27·2	43·1	52·7	60·1	45·2
1939	7·9	11·0	19·0	23·7	30·0	21·0
1950	4·9	6·0	10·5	13·9	18·8	11·2
(1950 rate as percentage of 1921)	32·7	22·1	24·4	26·4	31·3	24·8
Total under 1 year						
1921	38·4	55·5	76·8	89·4	97·0	79·1
1939	26·8	34·4	44·4	51·4	60·1	47·4
1950	17·9	22·2	28·1	33·7	40·7	29·3
(1950 rate as percentage of 1921)	46·6	40·0	36·6	37·7	42·0	37·0

* Carr-Saunders et al., op. cit., p. 222. More recent figures indicate a worsening of the position of class 5. See N. Butler and D. G. Bonham, *Perinatal Mortality*. London (1963).

The distinction between neonatal and post-natal deaths is important for consideration of the question of the role of genetic factors in accounting for these differences. Neonatal mortality is largely due to constitutional causes while post-natal is largely a reflection of environmental causes. In 1950 the class 5 neonatal rate was 70 per cent above

[1] A. Antonovsky, 'Social Class, Life Expectancy and Overall Mortality', *Milbank Memorial Fund Quarterly*, vol. 14, no. 2, 1967.

that for class 1, while the post-natal rate was *four times* as high. Obviously environmental causes are of greater weight in the production of the total disparity between the two; yet these figures would seem to assign a significant role to constitutional differences. However in a subsequent series of remarkable studies Illsley has shown how social processes combine with constitutional factors to produce differences in neonatal rates, particularly the processes of social mobility and selection of spouses.[1] Detailed medical and social data were obtained for some 4,344 *primiparae* resident and delivered in Aberdeen. It was found that 46 per cent of women brought up in classes 1 and 2 married men in class 3, while 40 per cent of women married to men in classes 1 and 2 were themselves brought up in class 3; 61 per cent of women brought up in classes 4 and 5 married into class 3, while 41 per cent of women married to men in classes 4 and 5 were brought up in class 3. Intermarriage between extreme classes is more rare. Forty-seven out of 648 women brought up in classes 1 and 2 marrried into classes 4 and 5, and only 56 out of 1,517 brought up in classes 4 and 5 married into classes 1 and 2. The important point is that Illsley also found that women who rise in social status at marriage tend to be of superior intelligence, education and occupational skill. They tend also to be tall, to be in good health and to have low prematurity and obstetric death rates. Conversely, women whose social status falls at marriage tend to have the opposite characteristics.

Illsley's findings tempt me to characterize the Registrar General's social classes as aristogynaecompetitive groups.[2] Class 5 receives other medically less sound types from the rest of the population. It has been noted since the twenties that it contained a relatively higher proportion of schizophrenics than other classes, and some students interpreted the finding in class-specific terms.[3] Goldberg and Morrison, however, have shown that it can be accounted for by the downward drift to labouring occupations of male schizophrenics from other classes who are unable to find or continue with the employment characteristics of their classes of origin.[4]

[1] R. Illsley, 'Social Class Selection and Class Differences in Relation to Stillbirths and Infant Deaths', *British Medical Journal*, 4 December 1955, pp. 1520–4.

[2] Viewed from this point of view, conspicuous consumption would be less a display of symbols of domination than a variety of sexual display of the sort some species put on at mating time. Perhaps the two aspects are closely connected. Compare the situation with that among the Tiwi and in caste society.

[3] For references and discussion on this and many other relations between class and health see M. W. Susser and W. Watson, *Sociology in Medicine*. OUP (1962).

[4] E. M. Goldberg and S. L. Morrison, 'Schizophrenia and Social Class', *British Journal of Psychiatry*, no. 109, pp. 785–802. For an anthropological comment on this see J. Littlejohn, *Twins, Birds*, etc., Bijdragen tot de Taal, Land en Volkenkunde (1970).

Education

The relation between stratification and education is one of the most thoroughly researched fields in British sociology, perhaps because it offers a good test case for examining the thesis of growing equality in capitalist society. Among the political philosophies claiming to represent the interests and aspirations of the working class, the dominant one in Britain conceives of equality as equality of opportunity. As the more highly paid occupations, it is argued, require longer education and training, the extent to which equality of opportunity has been realized can be estimated by the extent to which opportunity for secondary and higher education has beome available for all. Equal opportunity for higher education ought to result in high rates of mobility, offsetting disadvantages experienced by children of poor parents.

If there is one point on which all students of the relation between stratification and education agree it is that its outstanding feature is a process which rewards the middle class and deprives the working class. Although 25 per cent of university students were manual workers at the time of the Robbins Report (the same proportion as during the period 1928–47), only 2 per cent of the children of unskilled and semiskilled manual workers receive full-time higher education, compared with 45 per cent of the children of higher professional fathers.[1] Many relevant statistics and calculations have been brought together by Little and Westergaard; class differentials in educational opportunity, they write,

'result in the elimination of some 96 out of every 100 manual working class children before the age of 17. Moreover, as this process of elimination goes on, so the relative prospects of survival as between children of different social origin become steadily less equal. At 11–13 a professional or managerial family's child had nine times as high a chance of entering a grammar or independent school as an unskilled worker's child. Some years later, at 17, he had nearly thirty times as high a chance of still being at school'.[2]

However, the authors also make it clear that there has been during this century some reduction of inequality of educational opportunity, and considerable reduction in the sector of secondary school education. For those born before 1910 the ratio between the chances of entry to grammar school for class 1 and the chances for class 5 was 37 to 1. For the generation born in the late thirties the ratio was 6 to 1. Also, the magnitude of the disparity in chances cannot be entirely attributed

[1] Committee on Higher Education, *The Robbins Report*, HMSO (1963).
[2] A. Little and J. Westergaard, 'The Trend of Class Differentials in Educational Opportunity in England and Wales', *British Journal of Sociology*, no. 15, December 1964.

to a class discrimination process, but also to a sex discrimination process. Thus,

> 'an unskilled manual worker's daughter has a chance of only one in five or six hundred of entering a university: a chance a hundred times lower than if she had been born into a professional family'.[1]

Tables Twelve and Thirteen from Parkin's book help to put these figures in perspective.[2]

TABLE TWELVE

Percentage of university students of working class origin in European countries

Country	per cent
Great Britain	25
Norway	25
Sweden	16
Denmark	10
France	8
Austria	8
Netherlands	5
West Germany	5

TABLE THIRTEEN

Percentage of grammar school children of working class origin *circa* 1960

Country	per cent
Great Britain	52·0
Sweden	23·0
Netherlands	19·5
France	17·0
West Germany	16·0

That there is a long term trend towards increasing equality of opportunity in all sectors of education in the UK is agreed; what people disagree about is whether it proceeds at a satisfactory rate or not. It remains to examine the selective process. That the elimination of manual workers' children is not due either to a lower level of inborn ability among them (as measured by I.Q. tests), or even entirely to unsatisfactory academic performance during early years of schooling, has been shown by Douglas. Table Fourteen demonstrates the first point.

[1] A. Little and J. Westergaard, 'The Trend of Class Differentials in Educational Opportunity in England and Wales', *British Journal of Sociology*, no. 15, December 1964.
[2] E. Parkin, op. cit., pp. 110 and 112.

TABLE FOURTEEN

Social class by level of ability at age 11—percentage of 15-year-old children attending grammar, technical or independent schools*

Test score at 11 years	Middle class		Manual working class	
	Upper — At grammar, technical, or independent schools	Lower — At grammar, technical, or independent schools	Upper — At grammar, technical, or independent schools	Lower — At grammar, technical, or independent schools
	per cent	per cent	per cent	per cent
43–45	42·9	5·6	3·7	1·4
46–48	43·6	5·6	3·7	1·4
49–51	31·0	14·8	7·1	7·1
52–54	43·6	34·1	23·4	16·3
55–57	79·1	56·4	42·9	43·6
58–60	81·2	78·6	58·3	65·8
61–63	97·6	93·5	99·0	86·2
64–66	100·0	92·4	88·9	100·0
67 and over	100·0	98·8	97·8	100·0

* J. W. B. Douglas, op. cit., p. 181.

The second point is that districts vary tremendously in the number of places in grammar schools available in them.[1] Grammar school awards are seldom made on the results of intelligence tests alone, but also on results in school achievements tests and teachers' recommendations. Douglas found that where grammar school places are in short supply the upper middle class children are as likely to get grammar school places as they would be if they lived in more favoured areas, while in the poorly favoured areas the lower middle class children get 28 per cent fewer places than an equivalent (i.e. by I.Q. level and school achievement) group of upper middle class children: the upper manual working class children get 40 per cent fewer and the lower manual ones 48 per cent fewer.[2] In England many middle class children go to private secondary schools. When places in these are included in the calculations it emerges that, comparing children of equal measured ability at age eleven, children of the upper middle class get *three times* as many selective school places as those from the lower manual working class, twice as many as those from the upper manual working class, and one and a half times as many as lower middle class children.[3] Streaming by ability reinforces this selective process. Middle class children stand a greater chance of being initially put in the upper streams than their measured ability would seem to justify. Once there they are likely to stay and to improve in performance. In contrast children of measured ability, similar to those in A streams, who are placed in lower streams deteriorate in measured ability, especially the brighter ones.[4] Even the comprehensive school, created to provide for greater equality of opportunity among those, from both middle and working classes, of equal talent, does not necessarily do so. Ford shows that selection for streaming in the comprehensive school she studied underlines class differentials in educational opportunity, the middle class child still having a better chance of being permanently in the A stream.[5]

To speak of a selective bias in the system is liable to convey the impression of a middle class conspiracy against working class children. No doubt teachers sometimes, where marginal cases are concerned, favour middle class children in the allocation of pupils to stream or in recommending them for grammar school, though not necessarily with conspiratorial intent. It is possible that experience has taught them that a law of diminishing educational returns operates earlier and with greater force among working class children, for there is a

'consistent tendency of working class or manual workers' children

---

[1] See for example J. B. Mays, *Education and the Urban Child*. Liverpool (1962).   [2] Douglas, op. cit., p. 48.   [3] Ibid., p. 122.
[4] Ibid., chap. 14. See also B. Jackson, *Streaming: an Educational System in Miniature*. London (1964).
[5] J. Ford, *Social Class and the Comprehensive School*. London (1969).

to perform less well in school, and to leave sooner than the children of non-manual workers, even when they are of similar ability'.[1]

The tendency to leave sooner is apparent even if we consider forms of post-school education which provide an alternative to the grammar school-university route. The Crowther Committee, for example, found that middle class boys are more likely than their working class counterparts to go on to vocational part time courses and to complete a course once having started it.[2] Among 11-year-old children, class differentials in I.Q. score are well established, the class average steadily declining from class 1 to 5.[3] Douglas argues that since the difference between average manual and non-manual I.Q. scores increases over time the selective process itself has a deleterious effect on the test performance of the latter. It is an attractive idea both to those convinced (as any reasonable person must be, on reading Douglas' book) that there is a distribution of natural intelligence greatly at variance with its current social distribution and also to those convinced that in any case I.Q. tests, being composed by middle class intellectuals, merely test competence in middle class pursuits or the extent to which the child has internalized middle class values and norms. However, Douglas' argument has been contested by other researchers in the field, and his findings explained in other ways.[4]

Explanations for the underachievement of working class children have been sought mainly in the organization and attitudes of the working class family, in values and orientations held to be features of working class culture, as against middle class,[5] and to some extent in children's experiences in the local community or neighbourhood. As regards the latter, Jackson and Marsden, for example,[6] describe the tensions experienced by working class grammar school children as they find that to maintain the level of performance required of them they have to withdraw from the playgroups of the street or neighbourhood and sever friendships formed in childhood, only to perceive a cultural gap opening up between their parents and themselves.

Ideal type contrasts are frequently drawn between working class and middle class cultures. Thus, the working class have traditionally viewed society as a simple dichotomy of 'Them and Us' and they regard their social circumstances as largely a matter of luck which they must

[1] O. Banks, *The Sociology of Education*. Batsford (1968), p. 67.

[2] Ibid., pp. 55–7.

[3] Eds J. E. Floud *et al.*, *Social Class and Educational Opportunity*. Heinemann (1956).

[4] H. Horobin *et al.*, 'The Social Differentiation of Ability', *Sociology*, no. 1, 1957.

[5] On class cultures see J. Klein, *Samples from English Cultures*. London (1965). J. Littlejohn, *Westrigg*. London (1963).

[6] B. Jackson and D. Marsden, *Education and the Working Class*. London (1962).

make the best of. They think that they should not strive to achieve higher norms of consumption or explore new healms of culture, but simply maintain customary standards and live according to the current wisdom of the street. Action to promote or protect interests is typically collective action, and high value is set on group solidarity. One does not strive to differentiate onself. Parents aspirations for their children are modest, a trade or a steady job, and they do not encourage them to attain levels of education at which they would obtain jobs which would remove them from their class, if not their immediate families and community. It is more important to augment the immediate family budget, by sending children out to work, than to scrimp and suffer for a problematic future by keeping them at school. On the other hand, the middle class sees society as a kind of ladder and the individual as master of his fate, in so far as that is decided by his place on it. An individual has a duty to strive to move upwards, and to encourage his children to do so. The middle class see the present only in relation to some future personal goal which, in order to achieve, plans are consciously formulated and the possibilities of present gratification sacrificed. Individual achievement is approved of, where it is not envied, and parents, appreciating that education is a means towards it, encourage children to advance in educational progress.[1]

Perhaps the most celebrated contrast is that drawn by B. Bernstein of the use of language in the two classes.[2] He proposes that measurable differences in language ability, rather than simply reflecting differences in potential capacity, result from entirely different modes of speech characteristic of the two, which he calls formal and public languages. The formal language of the middle class is conceptual in character, analytic, and permits the elaboration of subjective intent and the definition of differences between speakers. The public language of the working class is concrete, descriptive, and prevents the elaboration of subjective intent, but establishes identification between speakers. Public language is grammatically simple, a language of nouns, short sentences, stereotyped traditional phrases, and 'sympathetic circularity', e.g. phrases like 'you see' or 'just fancy'. It is full of statements in which reason and conclusion are counfounded to produce categoric utterances. Formal language makes greater use of adjectives, adverbs, conjunctions and subordinate clauses, and in general is a more suitable vehicle for logical argument. Since teachers are exponents of formal language working class children are at a disadvantage in school compared with

---

[1] For studies drawn upon for such characterizations see Klein, op. cit.

[2] Probably the most concise statement of Bernstein's views is found in Bernstein, 'Social Class and Linguistic Development: a Theory of Social Learning', eds Floud et al., op. cit. For results of research based on his ideas see for example W. Brandis and D. Henderson, *Social Class, Language and Communication*. London (1970).

middle class children, who learn formal language at home. Bernstein has suggested, without exactly demonstrating, that public language is in some way connected with the structure of the working class family, and that it inhibits logical thought. His views have been found useful by educationists. However, it is perhaps as well to recognize that the prestige ranking of languages is altering rapidly at the moment, all word languages declining in status as against mathematical languages.

Such sharp contrasts, though useful as a preliminary guide to research, exaggerate differences by assuming homogeneity of culture and family life within each class, as all authors are aware. Bernstein, for example, is careful to stress that only the speech of the lower working class closely approximates to his account of public language. As regards more general culture, we have for example already noted differences between spiralists and burgesses in the middle class. Carter distinguishes four types of working class family in his study of the transition from school to work as experienced by the majority of working class children.[1] It has long been known that the children of skilled workers perform better at school than the children of unskilled workers. Some studies indicate that the most decisive influence of the working class child adopting a positive attitude to education, and on his chances of achieving a place in grammar school, is his or her mother. Mothers who foster a positive attitude and help their children achieve such a place by making demands of teachers and education authorities are likely to have some connection with the middle class, either through having been born into it or having had occupations before marriage superior to those of their husbands.[2] Again, it is well known that within each class children from large families tend not to do so well in I.Q. tests and scholastic examinations as children from small families. In short, we cannot account for the relatively poorer performance of working class children simply by reference to a working class culture, or to a family type held to be characteristic of the class. As Banks stresses, we need on this subject to know a great deal more about the general process of socialization.

As remarked, sociologists' interest in the education system has been motivated mainly by the wish to investigate the claim that it increasingly provides greater equality of opportunity, both as regards education itself and in consequence as regards subsequent employment. In promoting equality of opportunity it increases the volume of upward social mobility. That it does, to some extent, is not disputed,[3] but the extent to which it does is open to question. However we cannot estimate

[1] M. Carter, *Into Work*. Penguin (1966). *Home School and Work*. Pergamon Press (1962).

[2] Eds Floud *et al.*, op. cit. J. W. B. Douglas, op. cit.

[3] Ed. D. V. Glass, op. cit., chap. 10. See also S. Cotgrove, *Technical Education and Social Change*. London (1958).

the latter until we have more knowledge about overall rates and routes of mobility. Anderson's calculations led him to conclude that only a relatively modest part of all mobility is linked to education, there being far more mobility, both upward and downward, than can be explained in terms of education. Carlsson, from a study of Swedish data, similarly concluded that schooling is not a decisive factor in mobility, since about four-fifths of the subjects of both upward and downward mobility in the population studied had received only an elementary education.[1]

Available figures suggest that the USA provides opportunities for secondary and higher education for a larger proportion of working class children than do European countries, though the general pattern of class differences is much the same.[2] This is usually explained as due to the greater variety of institutions and courses available there, and to a mode of selection different from the European one, the two modes being in Turner's words, sponsored mobility and contest mobility.[3] The former resembles entry by sponsorship into a club. The elite closely supervise the process of ascent through the system, selecting their potential successors at an early age, segregating them in favoured institutions, imposing tests at various stages, and lacing the teaching of instrumental skills with indoctrination in the values and standards of elite culture. Contest mobility on the other hand resembles a race, in which all can compete. Early selection is avoided, competitors are not segregated, but they may drop out if they wish after having completed a required length of the course. The two are of course ideal types of mobility, but there is no doubt that the English white population, the latter.

Social mobility

Social mobility rates would probably provide the best measure of the overall distribution of life chances in any society. However, the assertion that social mobility rates are higher in industrial than pre-industrial societies is unverifiable, but unlikely to be true. It is unverifiable not only because we do not know what the rates were in most of those societies, but also because, for a variety of reasons, we are not very sure what they are in industrial societies, or even what exactly is to count as mobility.[4] It is unlikely to be true because we do know that

[1] A. C. Anderson, 'A Sceptical Note on Education and Mobility', eds Floud et al., op. cit., pp. 164–79. Ed. A. H. Halsey, *Education, Economy and Society.* Free Press (1961). G. Carlsson, *Social Mobility and Class Structure.* London (1958).   [2] Banks, op. cit., chap. 3.
[3] R. H. Turner, 'Modes of Social Ascent through Education', eds Floud et al., op. cit.
[4] For example, is rural depopulation in Britain a case of upward mobility? See for example Littlejohn, op. cit., chap. 8. For a treatment of mobility in a wide sense see I. Davies, *Social Mobility and Political Change.* London (1970).

mobility rates have been high, at least during certain periods in some pre-industrial societies. In caste society, with its high birth and death rates, the mobility rate through reincarnation must be quite enormous. Some recent studies of mobility in imperial China indicate high rates of mobility into the ranks of the bureaucracy.[1] There are always hard-faced men who do well out of wars and during the Wars of the Roses, for example, merchants ensconced themselves in large numbers in the ranks of the depleted aristocracy. If we are to judge from casualty lists in relation to the size of national populations then many of the battles in medieval times must have been followed by the swift recruit-ment of wealtheir peasants' sons into the ranks of the knights. Eduart Perray found that out of 215 noble lineages in a particular district of France in 1200, 66 had died out by 1300, and that the average duration of a noble line was only three to four generations. Poverty, a high death rate, war, political upheavals and the practice of sending younger sons into the church all contributed to this displacement of families, replaced from among richer men in non-noble strata as well as from junior branches of local and non-local noble families.[2] The rate of mobility from slave to freeman must have been considerable during the early decades of the principate, as indicated above. Generally speaking, rates of downward mobility from elite families are fairly high in pre-industrial societies.[3]

Most current studies of mobility attempt to measure rates or inci-dence of movement up and down the occupational hierarchy, par-ticularly across the manual/non-manual division. Two general types of mobility are distinguished, intragenerational and intergenerational, the former that which an individual accomplishes in his own lifetime, the latter that by which a child (sons in most studies) acquires a dif-ferent social status from his or her father. The extent of both is extremely difficult to measure,[4] but some findings from various studies are as follows.[5] Mobility has increased with economic growth, but most of it is due to the expansion of white collar and professional occupations coupled with a fertility rate among the former lower than that of

[1] For example, Ping-ti Ho, *The Ladder of Success in Imperial China: Aspects of Social Mobility 1368-1911*. N.Y. (1963).

[2] E. Perray, 'Social Mobility Among the French Noblesse in the later Middle Ages', *Past and Present*, no. 21, Apr. 1962. For a discussion of peasant mobility see J. A. Raftis, *Tenure and Mobility: Studies in the Social History of the Medieval English Village*. Toronto (1964).

[3] E. Lenski, op. cit.

[4] See O. Duncan, 'Methodological Issues in the Analysis of Social Mobility', eds N. J. Smelser and S. M. Lipset, *Social Structure and Mobility in Economic Development*. London (1966), pp. 51-97.

[5] Major sources are S. M. Lipset and R. Bendix, *Social Mobility in Industrial Society*. Heinemann (1959). S. M. Miller, 'Comparative Social Mobility', *Current Sociology*, no. 9 (1960). Ed. Glass, op. cit.

I

manual workers.[1] Rates, measured by intergenerational exchange
between manual and non-manual, are much the same for most
industrial societies, the USA in particular being no more open in this
respect than European societies. A percentage in the region of one-
third of sons move up and in most countries a slightly lower (but in
for instance Britain a higher) percentage move down. However, other
measures present a different picture. For example, rates of intergenerational mobility vary at different levels of the hierarchy and
countries differ with regard to these rates, also with regard to rates
of short and long range mobility. Most mobility in all countries is
short range, between adjoining strata, but while in Britain, for example,
skilled manual and routine non-manual workers have the highest
relative upward mobility of all status groups, mobility from the working
class into the higher professions and business elite is very much lower
than in the USA. Each country has its characteristic 'mobility profile'.[2]
Again, by constructing a measure of opportunity for sons of non-
manual fathers to remain in their parents' class as compared with
opportunity for sons of manual workers to move into non-manual
positions, Miller has shown that industrial societies differ markedly
in their degree of openness, as shown in Table Fifteen where the
lower the figure in the last column the higher the degree of openness.[3]

TABLE FIFTEEN

Country	Non-manual into manual	Manual into non-manual	Index of openness
Great Britain	57·9	24·8	234
Denmark	63·2	24·1	262
Sweden	72·3	25·5	284
Norway	71·4	23·2	308
France	79·5	30·1	264
Netherlands	56·8	19·6	290
Belgium	96·6	30·9	313
West Germany	71·0	20·0	355
Italy	63·5	8·5	747

As regards intragenerational mobility, the major finding is that:

'The overwhelming majority of those who start in a non-manual
occupation remain there, and the same applies to those who begin
their career as manual workers. For non-manual workers the proportion is 77 per cent for England, 87 per cent for Japan, 81 per
cent for Oakland, and 73 per cent for San Jose; for manual workers

[1] On class differentials in fertility see A. M. Carr-Saunders et al., op. cit.
[2] Miller, op. cit.
[3] Ibid.

the corresponding percentages are, England, 79; Japan, 74; Oakland, 65; and San Jose, 75'.[1]

Again there are variations at different levels, with the professions the least permeable by lower strata. For women one of the main if not the main avenue of intragenerational mobility is marriage, the wife's social status being dependent on that of her husband. In Britain, more women marry up than do men and the higher status groups are more endogamous than the lower.[2] The importance of education as an avenue of mobility for women is perhaps reflected in the fact that while in the cases analysed 45 per cent of marriages occurred between mates of similar social origins over 71 per cent occurred between mates of similar education levels.

I do not see by what criteria one can say that overall mobility rates in capitalist society are either high or low. As previously mentioned, upward social mobility has been viewed as a stabilizing element in capitalist society. Upward movement from lower strata, it is said, releases the successul individual from the frustrations of low status, weakens the solidarity of lower strata, and deprives them of their most able members who might otherwise lead them politically. It is also the case that there is a tendency for the upwardly mobile to change political allegiance from left to right-wing parties, and for the downwardly mobile and those threatened with downward mobility to become more right-wing in attitude.[3] Apart from the data on voting behaviour collected by Lipset there is no convincing evidence that these generalizations hold good, and even the data on voting behaviour is patchy.[4] Interpretation of the significance of mobility for the stability of social structure must, as with any judgement as to whether rates are high or low, await further research on what people expect in the way of mobility. The case of the affluent worker, discussed below, is relevant to this problem.

Power

So far we have been dealing with the dimensions of class and status. The dimension of power and its distribution is the most difficult to investigate, partly because of the vagueness of the concept, the virtual impossibility of measuring degrees of power, and the complexity of the power situation in modern capitalist society.[5] The complexity

---

[1] Lipset and Bendix, op. cit., p. 289.

[2] J. Berndt, in ed. Glass, op. cit., chap. 12.

[3] Lipset and Bendix, op. cit., pp. 64–72. S. M. Lipset, *Political Man*. N.Y. (1960). Davies, op. cit.

[4] K. H. Thompson, 'Upward Social Mobility and Political Orientation', *American Sociological Review*, no. 36, April 1971.

[5] See for example P. Warsley, 'The Distribution of Power in Industrial Society', *Sociological Review Monograph*, no. 8, 1964, pp. 15–41.

could be discussed in relation to three general issues. (*a*) The nation state is no longer (if it ever was) an independent entity, either economically or politically. International integration, though far from complete, imposes constraints on governments, particularly those of smaller countries such as Britain. International economic competition paradoxically requires that nations co-operate, i.e. accept rules limiting the autonomy of each one, to maintain the system within which competition is possible. The rules can be applied with greater force to the economically and politically weaker. So it is never certain who runs Britain—Wall Street, the International Monetary Federation, or the gnomes of Zürich, and so on. (*b*) Even granted that within Britain we regard the government of the day as the supreme repository of power, nevertheless a democratic government has to consider or make use of, in the formulation of policy, the opinion presented to it both by permanent bodies like the CBI, the TUC and civil service departments, and occasional enquiry units such as Royal Commissions.[1] Moreover around issues of some import, such as independent television authorities, there arise pressure groups. All these may be presumed to exercise power in some form at some time or another, though we cannot, without study of particular issues, ever know just how much. More important, because of these two situations, a mere enumeration of the members of the various classes in such bodies, a sketch of the anatomy of power, tells us little about the exercise of power, its physiology. (*c*) Even supposing we agree on a definition of power, how do we introduce it as a variable in an explanation of events, and particularly of non-events? For example, the distribution of private property in Britain would seem to indicate that the ruling class (in Marx's sense) still exercises a great deal of power otherwise it would have been unable to resist the attempts of the workers to achieve a more equitable distribution. However, as Lockwood points out:

> 'It is one thing to say that the property owning classes are still dominant because there wasn't a socialist revolution; but it is quite another thing to say that there wasn't a socialist revolution because of the dominance of the property owning classes.'[2]

Obviously I have not space to discuss these issues here. However, some figures on three *loci* of power may be taken to indicate, crudely, that the working class is virtually excluded from them.

It is well known that the higher the social class the higher is the percentage of Conservative voters in it, and the lower the class the higher the percentage voting Labour.[3] The Labour party represents,

---

[1] W. L. Guttsman, *The British Political Elite*. London (1963).

[2] D. Lockwood, 'The Distribution of Power in Industrial Society', *Sociological Review Monograph*, no. 8, 1964, pp. 35–41.

[3] See for example J. Blondel, *Voters, Parties and Leaders*. Penguin (1963). Eds P. Anderson and R. Blackburn, *Towards Socialism*. Fontana (1965).

or more nearly represents, or is the only one at present which might represent, the interests of the working class. Yet the chances of a working class person becoming a Labour MP have steadily declined over the century, as shown in Table Sixteen.

TABLE SIXTEEN

Percentage of Labour MPs of working class origin since 1918*

Year	per cent
1918–1935	72
1945	41
1951	45
1959	35
1964	30

* H. Glennerster, 'Democracy and Class', *More Power to the People*, eds B. Lapping and G. Radice. London (1968).

Recent Labour Cabinets, including shadow Cabinets, have been overwhelmingly composed of middle class MPs.[1]

Studies of recruitment into the highest level of the Civil Service, on the other hand, indicate that the proportion recruited from people born in the Registrar General's classes 3, 4 and 5 has increased a little since the First World War. However, the actual numbers so recruited are not large; in 1950 29·3 per cent were from class 1; 40·5 per cent from class 2, 24·2 per cent from class 3, and 3 per cent from classes 4 and 5.[2]

The third locus of power is the industrial elite. Copeman found that out of 1,243 directors of large public companies 51 per cent were sons of businessmen, the vast majority of the rest were sons of landowners, professional men or administrators, and only 8 per cent originated from classes 3, 4 and 5.[3] Some studies of managers, including lower levels hardly distinguishable from foremen, indicate that opportunities for promotion from the shop floor to management are diminishing precisely because of the demand for managers technically qualified through higher education.[4] Clements found that managers from higher social classes were promoted earlier and further, and on average had higher salaries than those from lower classes.[5]

It is well known that the working class is not united on the question as to who should govern Britain. Between 1886 and 1964 there were

[1] Blondel, op. cit., chap. 5. For European parties see Parkin, op. cit.
[2] R. K. Kelsall, *Higher Civil Servants in Britain*. London (1955).
[3] G. H. Copeman, *Leaders of British Industry*. London (1955).
[4] D. G. Clark, *The Industrial Manager: His Background and Career Pattern*. London (1966).
[5] R. V. Clements, *Managers: A Study of their Careers in Industry*. London (1958).

thirteen British elections, won on eleven occasions by the Conservative Party.[1] This, and the figures on MPs given above, raises the question as to why manual workers, who constitute a majority in the most heavily and longest urbanized and industrialized electorate of any democracy, fail to secure a greater share of power, whether by voting Labour or by supporting in local Party branches the nomination of manual workers as candidates. The fact that regularly about a third of manual workers vote for the Conservative Party, thereby providing them with about one half of their electoral support, does not explain, merely quantifies, the problem.[2]

On the subject of the nomination of candidates little is known except that the British electorate as a whole is indifferent to the elementary political procedures. Political activity in local branches is carried on by a tiny minority and accordingly, in this regard, manual workers merely conform to a basic norm of British political culture. The real problem is the working class Tory voter, about whom a certain amount has been discovered. This person is more likely than the working class Labour voter to be a woman, old, of low income, slightly more educated, an Anglican or Roman Catholic, descended from a non-manual father, not a member of a union, and to think of him or herself as belonging to the middle class.[3] That of course is to compose a caricature out of various factors which apparently have some bearing on the question. These factors have been analysed out of replies to questionnaires administered to a sample of voters. Many such voters are men, and MacKenzie and Silver find that the difference between working class Conservative and Labour voters is minimal as regards sex, income, and occupational skill level, but slightly more significant as regards age, in correlation with these other factors.[4] Runciman argues that self rated class, their identification with the middle class, is the most important variable explaning why they vote Conservative, but admits that this cannot be the complete explanation.[5]

Others offer an explanation in terms of British political culture, roughly as follows. The British nation is a deferential nation.[6] Britain's political development has

'allowed traditional attitudes to authority to become fused with more

---

[1] R. T. Mackenzie and A. Silver, 'The Delicate Experiment: Industrialism, Conservatism, and Working Class Tories in England', *Party Systems and Voter Alignments*, eds. S. M. Lipset and S. Rokkan. Free Press (1967).

[2] On class voting patterns in Britain see Blondel, op. cit., p. 57. For more general surveys see Lipset, op. cit., Alford, *Party and Society*. Chicago (1963).

[3] W. G. Runciman, *Relative Deprivation and Social Justice*. London (1966), chap. 4.

[4] Mackenzie and Silver, op. cit.

[5] Runciman, op. cit.

[6] W. Bagehot, *The English Constitution*. London (1919).

recent democratic values to form a governmental tradition in which leaders are expected to lead'.[1]

Conservative values pervade much of the working class: a feeling for hierarchy, that high status confers ability to govern, that governmental authority must not be questioned, only its mismanagement; and that national interests take precedence over class interests whatever the complexion of the ruling party. Deference voters, as they have been called,[2] are not anomalous, they are merely more firmly encapsulated in the general political ethos, preferring power to originate from an elite socially ascribed its position, expressing political judgements in terms of the personal character of leaders and not in terms of issues or policies, preferring continuity to abrupt change, and finally judging that the Conservative Party is the more patriotic one. The education system, particularly the segregation of leaders and led in public and state schools, and sponsored mobility, socialize children to accept the general ethos. In this connection it is interesting that some political scientists have recently questioned whether there is any very close connection between stratification and political behaviour, whether as Lipset put it:

'In every democracy conflict among different groups is expressed through political parties which, basically represent a democratic translation of the class struggle.'[3]

Sartori[4] for example is somewhat sarcastic about the notion that parties represent classes, pointing out that all we can legitimately say is that they may reflect classes, and enquiring why we should consider that England is a case of relatively pure class politics when a calculation of class voting[5] revealed an index of only 40 in the UK, 33 in Australia, 16 in the USA, and 6 in Canada. Dogan is similarly sceptical about the applicability of Lipset's proposition to France and Italy,[6] where religious affiliation is as important as class membership in determining voting patterns.

Studies in political culture are certainly illuminating, as are enquiries which seek, by questioning a nationally representative but scattered sample of individuals, to determine the factors influencing working

[1] G. A. Nordlinger, *The Working Class Tories*. London (1967).

[2] For a portrait see R. Samuel, 'The Deferential Voter', *New Left Review*, January 1960.

[3] Lipset, op. cit., p. 220.

[4] G. Sartori, 'From the Sociology of Politics to Political Sociology', *Politics and the Social Sciences*, ed. S. M. Lipset. OUP (1969).

[5] Correlating occupation and class position with voting behaviour. Constructed by Alford, op. cit.

[6] M. Dogan, 'Political Cleavage and Social Stratification in France and Italy', eds Lipset and Rokhan, op. cit.

class deferential voting. They have certain limitations. The notion of culture is not very helpful when we try to use it to understand variations in individual behaviour, but the other method on the other hand gives too much weight to the individual seen as composed of an aggregate of attributes, society itself being thus assumed to be a complex of attribute distributions rather than of systems of relationships. Some steps towards completing our picture of the working class Tory, by taking into account social relations, have been taken by Stacey and Lockwood.

Stacey found that in Banbury the population was divided into traditionalists and cosmopolitans (see page 110). Among the former both manual and non-manual workers conceived of stratification as a local status hierarchy, i.e. in terms of acceptance or rejection in local social relations. In the latter, non-manual workers conceived of strati-fication as a status hierarchy but different from the local one, while manual workers saw it as a division between two national categories with different attributes. Among manual workers, traditionalists tended to be employed in small, long-established local firms, cosmopolitans in large new ones. Differences between these two latter populations are reflecting in male voting, as shown in Table Seventeen.

TABLE SEVENTEEN

Party supporters in traditional and non-traditional firms compared*

| | Male household heads of known politics | | | |
| | Traditional firms | | Non-traditional firms | |
Group	Conservative or Liberal	Labour	Conservative or Liberal	Labour
Non-manual	72	13	36	18
Manual	47	54	89	233

* Stacey, *Tradition and Change*. OUP (1960).

The difference in political allegience between the two manual populations is obvious and striking. Stacey's findings and insights have been incorporated by Lockwood into a more general exposition of the connection between work place and community relationships, images of society, and political attitudes among manual workers, to which topic I now turn.

Images of society

Study of images of society is a kind of enquiry which cannot hope to produce results presentable in the apparently precise form that enquiry into distributions can achieve. Individuals differ widely in their images of society and some do not have any, or are unable to describe them.[1] However, sometimes all that is precise about the figures presented in statistical tables is the numbers. The significance of subjects' images of society for the study of stratification is that for the subjects their images have normative value, providing guides to behaviour and delimiting the horizons within which adaptations and attitudes are meaningful.

Early studies showed that most images are variations on two models of society, the one variously described as a hierarchical, prestige or status model, the other as a dichotomous, power or conflict model. In the first the system of stratification is seen as composed of layers differentiated by prestige, more or less correlated with income and education. In the second it is seen as in Ossowski's two class dependency model, sometimes with the stress on a conflict between them, sometimes on the powerlessness of the one as against the other. The first image was found to be more commonly held among the middle class, the latter more commonly among the working class.[2] In general that would seem to be the case, though as Hoggart shows manual workers' attitudes, even when they subscribe to a 'Them and Us' dichotomous model, are more various than that brief outline suggests.[3]

Lockwood has since identified three different working class models, correlated with differences in certain configurations of relationships which individuals are involved in through their work situation and the kind of community they live in.[4] First, a proletarian model, the dichotomous one, is typically found among those who work in industries like mining or docking in which propensity to strike is high.[5] Workers in these occupations are deeply involved in their jobs and in relations with workmates. The job, in addition to being the source of income, is viewed as a field for the display of masculine virtue, physical toughness and loyalty to mates.[6] The kind of community they inhabit is composed mostly of people like themselves and typically characterized by continuity of population over the generations, much intracommunity marriage, and consequent density of kinship ties among its members.[7] Mutual aid among neighbours is common. Associates in leisure time,

[1] See R. Popitz et al., Das Gesellschaftsbild des Arbeiters, for a discussion of the hazards in this kind of enquiry.

[2] A. Willener, Images de la Société et Classes Sociales. Bern (1957).

[3] R. Hoggart, The Uses of Literacy. London (1957), chap. 3.

[4] D. Lockwood, 'Sources of Variations in Working Class Images of Society', Sociological Review, no. 14, November 1966.

[5] C. Kerr and A. Siegel, 'The Inter-Industry Propensity to Strike: An International Comparison', A. Kornhauser et al., Industrial Conflict. London (1954).

[6] See for example J. Tunstall, The Fishermen. London (1965). N. Dennis et al., Coal is our Life. London (1956).

[7] M. Young and P. Willmott, op. cit.

characterized by a gregarious sociability among men and segregation of the sexes, are also workmates. Conversation is mostly about the job, and beer drinking has a sacramental quality, affirming the loyalties and sentiments generated at work and in the community. The obverse of this solidarity is a collective hostility to 'Them', the white collar managers and clerks, the public officials in local bureaucracies who do not share the daily toil of manual workers nor their leisure, but who on the other hand give orders at work to manual workers, or otherwise 'push them around'. Voting Labour, as they mostly do, is simply the political expression of this hostility. Second, is the hierarchical model such as Stacey describes for traditionals who typically inhabit a small community of mixed class composition with a well defined local hierarchy. The typical employment of the manual worker is in a small family firm, farm or estate, where a personal relationship between employer and employee masks or ameliorates potential conflict between them. Those above him in status he sees as his betters, those at the top as natural leaders. Since Conservative MPs are almost without exception of higher status than himself,[1] he is inclined to vote Tory.

These two types of worker are both highly integrated into local communities, are found in industries which are declining in relative importance, and, both having a keen sense of belonging to a group, see strata

'as active social formations and not merely as amorphous aggregates of individuals'.[2]

In all that, they differ markedly from the typical worker who views society in terms of the third model, a pecuniary one. He sees class divisions as differences in income and material possessions only. The vast majority of people, both manual and non-manual, comprise a collection of ordinary people among whom he counts himself. A small minority are different in being very rich, and another in being very poor. Neither status nor power are axes of differentiation. His typical occupational habitat is the large factory with a mass production technology in which work is devoid of interest and so organized that close relationships with workmates is impossible. Work is merely a means of acquiring an income for real life elsewhere. He adopts a purely calculating attitude to relations with managers and employers, attempting always to maximize wages, and views his union not as a political association or, as was the case in early days and in a few cases still is, a source of fellowship,[3] but simply as his spokesman in bargaining. His community life is as desocialized, or 'privatized' in Lockwood's

[1] Blondel, op. cit.
[2] Lockwood, op. cit.
[3] I. C. Cannon, 'Ideology and Occupational Community', *Sociology*, May 1967.

phrase, as his work life, his typical territory being the council low-cost housing estate in which thousands of families live side by side without involving themselves in a gregarious and intense sociability. Large numbers of them have been geographically mobile, kinship ties among them are few, and no value is ascribed to neighbourliness. In so far as he is made aware of status differences it is merely through invidious comparison of levels of consumption among coresidents, which process carries with it no sense of membership in a definite group or of belonging to a category with clear cut boundaries. Hence in his view stratification has nothing to do with social relationships and differences among people are purely quantitative. The industries he is typically found in are new and expanding and wages are relatively high, thus attracting immigrants from less favoured areas. Some of these are of non-manual origin, and tend to vote Conservative. The majority how-ever vote Labour, though not as an expression of the class solidarity prompting the proletarians to do so, but simply because they see the Labour Party as the one most likely to bring about improvement in their standard of living.

These types of workers and models are ideal-typical constructs, doubtless subject to qualification in particular instances. For example, an obvious question concerning the linkage Lockwood postulates between deferential voting and low position in a well defined local hierarchy is that there are surely not now so many manual workers in such a position as to account for the working class Tory vote. This is true, but a large proportion of that vote is female, and women are not involved in relationships of opposition to each other in the world of employment.[1] The configuration of daily relationships that women are, for the most part, involved in hardly motivates them to adopt a dichotomous model of society. Representative data from which the first two models are drawn has been cited above; data from which the third is drawn comes largely from studies of the affluent worker, con-sidered below. Meanwhile we may note that few if any sociologists contest the view that a radical and militant class consciousness has been declining among manual workers over at least the last three decades, though not all agree that the instrumental collectivism of the privatized worker as described by Lockwood is to be regarded as having permanently replaced it.[2] Runciman regards his findings on relative deprivation, the discrepancy between the facts of massive inequality in our society and manual workers' relatively weak feelings of deprivation, as evidence of that decline. For example, when manual workers are asked questions aimed at eliciting whether or not they feel satisfied with their incomes relative to other people's, the reference groups they use for the purpose of comparison are mostly chosen

[1] Littlejohn, op. cit.
[2] See the essays by Westergaard and Anderson, op. cit.

from among those people close to their own situation and not usually from among non-manual workers, far less the very rich.[1]

Embourgeoisement and the affluent worker[2]

Diverse processes and enquiries during the decade 1950–60 seemed to lend support to the thesis of the embourgeoisement of some sectors of the British working class. The narrowing of pay differentials between some sections of the white collar work force and some sections of the manual during this period has already been mentioned. The decade also witnessed an impressive improvement in the living standards of manual workers, as measured by better housing, increase in home ownership and possession of domestic equipment such as the washing machine, television and car.[3] Several studies of workers and working class communities indicated that the change in standard of living was accompanied by changes in norms and style of life. Thus Young and Willmott described the social life of the manual workers of Bethnal Green much in the terms used above for the proletarian type of worker. Widespread and close knit networks are used in mobilizing mutual aid, in celebrating marriages, christenings or birthdays, and in mourning the dead; there is separation of the sexes in leisure, male indifference to domestic tasks and men's gregarious pub sociability, a sentiment of community unity and of opposition to non-manual workers. When, however, Bethnal Green families moved to new housing estates in Greenleigh new norms emerged. The nuclear family was rehoused as an independent unit, and most families were strangers to each other. Ties of kinship and neighbourhood no longer bound residents together, mutual aid between neighbours was no longer practised, there was no community sentiment, men spent less time and money, or none at all, in pubs and instead bought new furniture and household equipment, and took more interest in domestic tasks and the rearing of children. The former Bethnal Greeners became part of the 'home centred society',[4] in which householders, far from being neighbours in the traditional sense, vied with each other in consumption of commodities. Other researches indicated that the change was by no means confined to emigrants from Bethnal Green to Greenleigh.[5]

During the decade the British Labour Party was defeated in three elections and on each occasion their share of the poll fell. Psephological analysis of some polling results indicated that the decline in Labour's support was greatest in areas characterized by large-scale rehousing projects and the presence of the more technologically and economically advanced industries. The inference drawn was that the better housed

---

[1] Runciman, op. cit.   [2] Goldthorpe *et al.*   [3] Ibid., p. 22.
[4] M. Abrams, 'The Home Centred Society', *The Listener*, 26 November 1959.
[5] See J. Klein, op. cit., chap. 5.

and higher paid manual workers were withdrawing their support from Labour and giving it to the party of the middle classes.[1] To many these various processes, economic, demographic, social and political, seemed to be interconnected and explicable only by the hypothesis that a large proportion of the working class had become middle class; indeed the view received governmental endorsement.[2]

However, as Goldthorpe and Lockwood point out, the proponents of the view never made clear what exactly the changes in our system of stratification were that they wished to explain by the concept of embourgeoisement. They distinguish three possibilities corresponding to three aspects of stratification, economic, normative and relational: (a) the acquisition by manual workers of incomes and houses comparable to those of some non-manual workers; (b) the adoption by manual workers of a distinctively middle class life style; (c) the acceptance by the middle class of manual workers as associates of equal status to themselves.[3]

Some figures collected by Runciman in his 1962 survey give some indication of the relative economic position of manual and non-manual strata, as shown in Table Eighteen.

TABLE EIGHTEEN

Distribution of personal incomes among respondents in Runciman survey*

	Non-manual	Manual
Income per week	per cent	per cent
Over £20	26	1·6
Over £15	47	13
£10–£15	31	38
£10 and under	22	49

* From Runciman, op. cit., pp. 190–1. The figures were compiled from respondents' estimates of their after-tax incomes.

The overlap between the two was greater when household income was considered, as shown in Table Nineteen.

The difference in distribution of the two sorts of incomes indicates some of the costs manual workers pay for the relative gains in prosperity they have won, particularly the withdrawal of children from education

[1] D. E. Butler and R. Rose, *The British General Election of 1959*. London (1960).

[2] F. Zweig, *The Worker in an Affluent Society*. London (1961). Central Office of Information, Social Changes in Britain, December 1962. Klein, op. cit., p. 420.

[3] J. H. Goldthorpe and D. Lockwood, 'Affluence and the British Class Structure', *Sociological Review*, no. 11, 1962.

and a higher proportion of working wives than in the middle class (40 per cent as compared with 29 per cent). Goldthorpe and his colleagues found some other costs. Comparing men of the two classes in three large firms known for high wages, job security, advanced technology and progressive employment policies, they found that three-quarters of the manual workers were on shift work and on average worked 50 hours per week. Few white collar workers, on the other hand, were on shifts or overtime, and their average working week was 38·5 hours. The level of job satisfaction among manual workers was lower than among non-manual. Clearly, the work situation and experience of the former was not typical of that of the middle class, however affluent they might be.

TABLE NINETEEN

Distribution of household incomes among respondents in Runciman survey*

	Non-manual	Manual
Income per week	per cent	per cent
Over £20	36	12
Over £15	59	32
£10–£15	25	35
£10 and under	16	33

* From Runciman, op. cit., pp. 190–1. The figures were compiled from respondents' estimates of their after-tax incomes.

Regarding relations between members of the two classes, the authors found, as numerous other researchers have,[1] that there was little social interaction between even the most affluent manual workers and the white collar workers. There was no evidence either that manual workers particularly *wanted* to be accepted as associates by the middle class. As indicated in the account of their typical image of society, for them class has nothing to do with social relations, only money. Hence their acquisition of some of the domestic equipment hitherto possessed only by classes above them cannot be interpreted as a striving for higher status on their part. The author's findings with regard to the political allegiance of affluent workers (described under the privatized image) also did not support the thesis of embourgeoisement, but on the other hand it did indicate that their allegiance to Labour is different in nature from that of the proletarian worker.

The researchers found no evidence of affluent workers adopting norms considered characteristic of a middle class life style. Choosing

[1] See for example M. Young and P. Willmott, *Family and Class in a London Suburb*. London (1960).

friends from outside one's network of kin and immediate neighbours, entertaining friends in the home, and membership of voluntary associations are commonly held by sociologists to be features of that life style, but these were not features of the affluent worker's life-style. On the other hand, they were not features of the life style of lower paid clerks either. It follows that either (a) sociologists do not know very much about middle class life styles, and have assumed that norms characteristic of one section of the middle class are characteristic of all sections, or (b) lower paid members of the middle class have recently become privatized, so that such normative convergence as is evident is due not only to changes in working class life but also to changes in middle class life and experience. The great increase in membership of white collar unions over the last decade might be seen as evidence of such a process of convergence. C. W. Mills had suggested in 1951 that clerical workers would develop a different life style from that of the established middle class, by way of adaptation to low income and as a result of their subjection to the processes of bureaucratization and rationalization at work.[1]

It is clear at any rate that the decline in working class radicalism cannot be attributed to large numbers of them having become middle class, in the total way suggested by the theory of embourgeoisement, through affluence. Indeed, the more affluent workers studied by Goldthorpe and his colleagues show higher than average support for Labour.[2] Another kind of explanation is associated with elite theory. Working class leaders, it is argued, whether in political parties or trade unions become powerful bureaucrats separated by the nature of their functions, their power and relatively high incomes from the workers themselves. They may often adopt a middle class life style; in any case they become more interested in maintaining the bureaucratic machines and their own exalted position in them than in representing the interest of the workers in a radical transformation of society.[3] As they temper their demands on industry and the state to a level that entails no drastic change in the *status quo*, so they are easily absorbed into the apparatus of government. Thus in Britain in 1939 union leaders were represented on only twelve government committees, by the 1950s on over eighty.[4] Having thus accepted responsibility for maintaining the *status quo* they can no longer pursue radical policies. Simultaneously, aspiring politicians from the non-propertied middle class,[5] who can always be trusted to spot a good bandwagon when they see it, begin to

[1] C. W. Mills, *White Collar*. OUP (1951).
[2] J. Goldthorpe *et al*. *The Affluent Worker: Political Attitudes and Behaviour*. Cambridge (1968).
[3] R. Michels, *Political Parties*. N.Y. (1962).
[4] V. L. Allen, *Militant Trade Unionism*. London (1966), p. 51.
[5] On the different background of Conservative and Labour middle class MPs see Blondel, op. cit., p. 141.

join erstwhile radical parties and take command of them. This some-what cynical view accordingly proposes that radicalism declines through the embourgeoisement of working class leadership.

Another argument which postulates divergence of interest between leaders and led, but which owes more to observation of certain tendencies in the economy and industrial organization, is this. The main function of a trade union is to fix, with employers, the wage rate for a category of workers throughout a whole industry. An industry, however, is an abstraction and production is carried on in plants, owned by several companies, scattered over the country. Plants differ in production rates, in specialized production lines, in size and com-position of labour force, and in the local conditions, such as supply of labour, that managers have to reckon with in planning. Managers accordingly compete in attracting labour by offering payments in excess of the national wage rate which thereby becomes merely a minimum wage below which payments never fall. Excess payment may take several forms such as bonuses or opportunities for overtime. Local agreements over payment entail purely local bargins within a plant, and disputes about their implementation cannot be dealt with by the union, empowered to act only on a national basis. Most industrial disputes are in fact about conditions and payments within particular plants, and those who represent the workers within a plant are the shop stewards, who are not union officials. Hence unions no longer represent the vital interests of the workers. This, while accounting for the oft noted fact that British workers are more militant at the shop floor or industrial level than at the national political level, hardly explains the decline of political militancy itself. Moreover, precisely because industrial militancy is as evident in nationalized industries as in private, and because the state guarantees the legitimacy of bargins arrived at between unions and employers, the distinction between industrial and political militancy is not altogether clear cut.[1]

The most radical and original explanations for the decline of the latter are those given by neo-Marxists such as Marcuse, starting from a concept of alienation and the international political situation, dominated by conflict (or threat of it) between Russia and America. Whether or not in the future further development within the two results in convergence of their social systems, it is clear that at present they differ in crucial respects, particularly as regards stratification. Our information on inequalities in the Soviet Union is not very extensive, but we do know that occupations are ranked and differentially rewarded in wages and prestige.[2] To what extent differential rewards combine with inheritance

[1] M. Kidron, *Western Capitalism since the War*. Penguin (1970), chap. 5.

[2] Inkeles and Rossi, 'National Comparisons of Occupational Prestige', *American Journal of Sociology*, vol. 61, 1956. Eds. A. Inkeles and K. Geiger, *Soviet Society*. N.Y. (1961).

(of wealth, social status or a culture conferring advantage in competition for the best jobs) as in capitalist society to form strata is not exactly known. However, even if we grant with the functionalists that mere differential distribution of rewards constitutes stratification there remains a major difference. In capitalist society the crucial stratifying agencies are unequal distribution of property and market forces, while in Soviet society the Communist Party is the main such agency, regulating wage rates and recruitment into occupations, including the higher reaches of the Party itself.[1] Stratification is *politically* regulated, either in the interests of a national plan for increasing production or of the Party in maintaining its dominant position,[2] or both.

Yet on another plane the two societies are already so similar that nothing but an iron curtain (and not, for instance, belief in different gods) could separate them. In both the world is conceived as a system of energy and man's main task as the location and utilization of it, a task requiring that he conceive of himself as a source and consumer of energy. Both are accordingly dominated by the concepts of positive science and the massive technological apparatus in which they achieve actual existence, and in both men submit to the exigencies of operating it. Though that submission entails subjection to continuous processes of rationalization men accept this subjection, partly because the rulers in each, commanding the mass media, persuade their subject populations that their only protection against being annihilated by the other is to produce ever more military hardware; partly because men are alienated anyway, not as workers in the nineteenth century were by insecurity, starvation and exclusion from public life, but in the first place by comfort, by having all material needs satisfied. They are also alienated through being deprived of any language in which possible alternatives to present social actuality could be formulated. Criticism is impotent before the comfort achieved by the worker, permission to drop out and rot (capitalism), the threat of the psychiatric ward or the labour camp (communism), and the sheer power of modern technology, which transforms every item of former cultures into instruments of domination. Even the street is no longer where public life erupts, but a motorway for industry, the consumer or the tank corps. Marcuse is pessimistic about the possibility of any change in the foreseeable future. At the time of writing, however, the prospects for capitalism are not as rosy as they seemed a decade ago.

[1] J. H. Goldthorpe, 'Social Stratification in Industrial Society', op. cit.
[2] M. Djilas, *The New Class*. London (1957).

K

SUBJECT INDEX

capitalism, 14 ff., 20 ff., 41, 63 ff.,
    Ch. 5
caste, 13, Ch. 4
citizenship, 50, 96
civil servants, 112, 133
class, 12, 14, 20, 23, 32, 34, 37, 44 ff.,
    87 ff., Ch. V
commodity, 16 ff.
Conservative, 111, 132 ff.
conspicuous consumption, 29, 120
contradiction, 14, 91

education, 121 ff.
elite, 49, 95, 97
embourgeoisement, 29, 140
equality, 9 ff., 18, 112 ff.
exchange, 16 ff., 42 ff., 82 ff.

family, 33, 34, 46, 52, 63, 76, 121,
    125, 137, 141
functionalism, 11, 30 ff., 41 ff., 89 ff.,
    101

history, 15, 21, 25, 27

ideology, 12, 15, 19, 38, 86, 136 ff.,
    145
income distribution, 115
industrialization, 67, 88, 98 ff.

jajmani system, 82 ff.

Labour, 111, 132, 136, 138 ff., 141,
    143
Life chances, 27, 118 ff.

market, 15, 18, 23, 61, 64, 83, 91, 96

middle class, 61, 93, 101, 106, 108,
    111, 116, 118, 121 ff., 129 ff., 141

natural law, 11, 18, 66

occupational ranking, 34, 41, 73,
    105 ff., 144

pollution, 70 ff., 86
power, 21, 28, 31, 33, 60, 79, 98, 105,
    131 ff.

race, 58, 63 ff., 85 ff., 110
radicalism, 92, 100, 133 ff.
rationalization, 27, 145
rebellion, 59 ff.
revolution, 12, 59 ff., 91, 132

slavery, 18, Ch. 3
social development, 11 ff.
socialization, 111, 127, 136 ff.
social mobility, 33, 57, 66, 76, 80, 89,
    99, 128 ff.
social structure, 38, Ch. 2
status, 23, 29, 32, 47, 58, 64, 76, 99,
    109
status group, 23 ff., Ch. 4, 110, 112

theory of convergence, 28, 99, 144
trade unions, 14, 117, 134, 138, 143

values, 26, 30 ff., 51, 70, 89

working class, 12, 16, 20, 41, 93, 97,
    100, 106, 111, 116, 118 ff., 121 ff.,
    129, 133 ff., 137 ff.

AUTHOR INDEX

Abrams, M., 97, 140
Adorno, T. W., 30
Alford, A., 134, 135
Allen, V. L., 143
Althusser, L., 139
Anderson, A. C., 128
Anderson, P., and Blackburn, R., 132
Andrews, A., 56
Antonovsky, A., 119
Arendt, H., 51, 60
Arensberg, C. M., 76
Aron, R., 13, 94, 98, 99
Augustine, St, 59

Bagehot, W., 134
Bailey, F. C., 69, 80, 86
Banks, M., 78
Banks, O., 125, 129
Baran, P., 41
Barber, B., 31, 34, 45, 89
Barker, E., 56
Barrow, R. H., 57, 65
Bateson, G., 59
Bauer, A., 101
Bell, C., 111
Bell, D., 89, 100
Bendix, R., 100
Bernard, J., 101
Berndt, J., 131
Bernstein, B., 126
Berreman, G. D., 76, 79, 86
Bétaille, A., 47, 75, 77, 86, 88
Birnbaum, N., 96, 111
Blackburn, R., 104, 113, 114
Blauner, R., 100
Bloch, M., 63
Blondel, J., 132, 133, 134, 138, 143
Bott, E., 105
Bottomore, T., 2, 37, 97, 112, 117
Bottomore, T., and Rubel, M., 49
Bouglé, C., 77, 79
Brandis, W., and Henderson, D., 126
Buckley, W., 46
Burnham, J., 98
Burns, T., and Stalker, G., 76
Butler, D. E., and Rose, R., 141

Cannon, I. C., 138
Carcopino, J., 62

Carlsson, G., 128
Carr-Saunders, A. M. et al., 103, 118, 130
Carstairs, G. M., 81
Carter, M., 127
Clark, D. G., 133
Clements, R. V., 133
Cohn, B. S., 81
Cole, G. D. H., 92
Copeman, G. H., 133
Cotgrove, S., 127
Cowell, F. R., 53, 59
Cox, O., 85

Davies, I., 128
Davis, K., and Moore, W. E., 30, 34
Dahrendorf, R., 36, 38, 95, 97
Dennis, N. et al., 137
Djilas, M., 145
Dogan, M., 135
Douglas, J., 107, 109, 112, 123
Douglas, M., 70
Dube, S., 74
Dumézil, G., 72
Dumont, L., 66, 68, 71, 72, 74, 76, 81, 86, 89
Duncan, O., 129

Elkins, S. M., 66
Engels, F., 14
Epstein, T. S., 73, 80, 84–5

Fei, H., 52
Feinstein, C. H., 114
Finley, M. I., 49, 52, 56
Firth, R., 18, 62, 84
Floud, J. et al., 125, 127
Ford, J., 124
Forsyth, M., 113
Frank, T., 62

Galbraith, K., 96, 100
Geiger, T., 97
Glass, D. V., 106, 127, 129
Goldberg, E. M., and Morrison, S. L., 120
Goldthorpe, J. H., 100, 145
  et al., 29, 102, 109, 140, 143
  and Lockwood, D., 141